PORSCHE
924

www.veloce.co.uk

First published in 2000 by Veloce Publishing Limited, Veloce House, Parkway Farm Business Park, Middle Farm Way, Poundbury, Dorchester, Dorset, DT1 3AR, England.
Fax 01305 250479/e-mail info@veloce.co.uk/web www.veloce.co.uk or www.velocebooks.com.
This edition first printed May 2016. ISBN: 978-1-845849-77-1 UPC: 6-36847-04977-5

PORSCHE

BRIAN LONG

VELOCE PUBLISHING
THE PUBLISHER OF FINE AUTOMOTIVE BOOKS

PORSCHE 924

INTRODUCTION AND ACKNOWLEDGEMENTS

In many ways, the 914 represented a complete departure from the traditional Porsche line, but its replacement - the 924 - moved the marque into completely new territory. The 924, which was designed by Porsche but actually commissioned by Volkswagen, featured a water-cooled engine situated at the front of the vehicle. This entry-level model was exactly what Porsche needed in the mid-1970s, an uncertain time of industrial disputes, rising prices and cutbacks.

However, the 924 was not only about economy, as the 924 Turbo, introduced at the end of 1978, had the performance one expects from a Porsche. In addition, the 924 had an impressive record on the race track, not only in Europe but America, too. The model even made appearances on the Monte Carlo and Safari Rallies. The Carrera GT, then the GTS and GTR, kept alive the great Porsche tradition of proving all its models in competition.

The 924 Turbo gave way to the 944, but the normally-aspirated 924 soldiered on into the summer of 1988. By this time it was known as the 924S and was fitted with the 2.5 litre engine from the 944.

Like the 914 before it, the 924 remained underrated for many years. Nowadays, however, its qualities are at last being appreciated. This is the full history of the model; the background behind its introduction, development in the European and North American markets, and its demise.

Once again, the factory in Stuttgart has been extremely helpful in supplying information and photographic material. As with my previous two Porsche books written for Veloce, the vast majority of pictures have been sourced from the works' archives.

Of the many people that have helped with this project, I would like to thank Klaus Parr at Porsche AG in particular, not only for his unfailing support - I think it would be impossible to find anyone with a closer bond to the company they work for - but for being a good friend outside of office hours as well. I would also like to single out Jens Torner, Klaus' assistant, for his help on the photographic side.

Brian Long
Chiba City, Japan

CONTENTS

PORSCHE 924

1

A BRIEF HISTORY OF THE MARQUE

By the late 1920s, Professor Ferdinand Porsche's reputation as a designer was unrivalled in Germany. He had worked for Lohner, Austro-Daimler, Daimler (which soon became Daimler-Benz) and Steyr. After leaving the latter concern, however, he felt the time had come to establish his own company.

Registered in April 1931, a design studio was set up in Stuttgart with a team of hand-picked engineers and designers. This team included Porsche's son, Ferry, who was then just 21 years old. Ferry Porsche inherited much of his father's natural flair for engineering, and, although he wanted to become a racing driver, his father believed that Ferry's real talents lay in engineering and design and soon put a stop to this aspiration. This is perhaps fortunate for, without him, the Porsche company, as it exists today, would never have evolved, and neither would the vehicles recognized as the 'true' Porsches.

Adolf Hitler was very supportive of German industry, and financed the Mercedes-Benz and Auto Union racing programmes to show the world the strength of German engineering. The highly-successful Auto Union V16 Grand Prix car was a Porsche design,

The Lohner-Porsche, which achieved a surprising amount of competition success. This is the first one built, dating from 1900.

Porsche also designed the V16 Auto Union Grand Prix car, one of the vehicles that formed the basis of the Silver Arrows legend.

of course, but it was the Volkswagen project which provided the basis for the Porsche success story. The Volkswagen was also financed by the Nazi Party – a blessing at the time, but one which would cause problems later.

Just as Hitler was approving the final plans for the Volkswagen, the Second World War broke out. During the hostilities, Porsche and his team were moved to the Austrian village of Gmünd, and there they produced many designs, including those for a number of tanks. Professor Porsche was arrested and interrogated by the Allied authorities after the war, because of his "links" with the Nazi leader. He was promptly released, however, and went to France to work for Renault. Whilst there, Porsche and his son-in-law, Anton Piech, were arrested and imprisoned by the French on war criminal charges, with a ransom of one million francs. Ferry Porsche had also been imprisoned for a short time, but his sister, Louise Piech, had managed to negotiate his release.

With the Porsche offices in Stuttgart occupied by the United States Army, Ferry Porsche had little chance of raising the ransom money required for the release of his father (he was merely repairing ex-Army Volkswagens at this time). By an amazing stroke of luck, however, Ferry was approached by Carlo Abarth (the famous engine tuner) and Piero Dusio, a rich Italian industrialist who, amongst other things, wanted to build a Grand Prix car.

The Cisitalia, as it was known, drew heavily on the pre-war Auto Union designs, and was very complex. The project was sadly destined to fail, as escalating costs put a potentially successful car out of the reach of even Dusio's wealth. Nonetheless, it did provide Ferry Porsche with enough money to free his father. The Professor was allowed back to Austria in August 1947, but died less than four years later. His health had never been the same following his imprisonment, but at least he was able to see his son develop a new car bearing the family name.

The legendary 356
Design work on the Type 356 sports car had begun in Gmünd after Ferry Porsche decided that his small company should construct a vehicle

Ferry Porsche (left) and his father pictured with Porsche Number One of 1948.

A fascinating photograph of the prototype Porsche coupé, with (from left to right) Edwin Kaes, Ferdinand Karl Piech and Michael Piech. Ferdinand Piech, Ferry Porsche's nephew, would later be a key figure in the Porsche and Volkswagen-Audi story.

based on Volkswagen components. The first drawing was dated 17 July 1947, just one month after the project was instigated.

The first chassis was completed in March 1948, and fitted with a prototype open body two months later. The spaceframe chassis on Number One was well designed, but unsuitable for cost-effective series production as it was very labour-intensive to build.

The engine was a tuned 1131cc Volkswagen unit mounted back to front to give good weight distribution; unfortunately, it took up too much space to allow for any more than two seats. A number of other problems were encountered with this set-up and, from the second car onwards, the engine was mounted in traditional Volkswagen fashion on a sheet steel platform chassis.

Number One was taken to the European Grand Prix in Switzerland to allow journalists to try the car, and it was at this meeting that Porsche met Rupprecht von Senger, who was particularly enthusiastic. Von Senger and his partner agreed to buy the next four cars, and were very helpful in getting supplies from Wolfsburg to Gmünd.

The second car was a coupé, completed in August 1948. Aerodynamics were very good and, combined with the lack of openings at the front and the seamless construction of the body, meant that the Porsche was capable of some very high speeds for such a small-engined car.

Announced during the summer of 1948, the car's public debut was scheduled for the Geneva Show in 1949. It wasn't long before a 1086cc capacity was chosen, allowing the cars to compete in the 1100cc Class at international level. Meanwhile, in mid-September 1948, Porsche sealed a deal with Volkswagen securing the supply of parts, as well as use of the Volkswagen dealer and service network.

The Gmünd cars were completely handbuilt, their aluminium bodies being beaten into shape as there simply wasn't the money available to tool up. According to Ferry Porsche, 46 cars were built at Gmünd between June 1948 and March 1951. However, figures vary wildly between sources, with most quoting 50 or 51 vehicles.

Serious production began early in 1950 when the firm moved back to Stuttgart. The Porsche site was still being used by the Americans at the time, so the factory belonging to Porsche's neighbours – the Reutter body works – was used initially.

8

Reutter had been given the contract to build new steel bodies for Porsche in November 1949, and an area was set aside for the motor manufacturer.

The first steel-bodied Porsche was completed in April 1950. There were a number of differences to the Gmünd alloy cars, but they were subtle. In fact, mild and constant updating was to become a feature of Porsche production, as the company preferred to introduce new models that were evolutions of the outgoing vehicle. Even competition Porsches were largely based on production cars during these early days.

Ferry Porsche – creator of a legend.

A display of Porsches from the opening months of 1954, seen here as part of a special exhibition held at a Volkswagen dealership. The 550 Spyder (centre stage) was actually an early prototype disguised as one of the 1954 Mille Miglia cars.

A 356 cabriolet from 1955 – the final year of the pre-A models.

At the 1950 Paris Show, an ailing Ferdinand Porsche held talks with Max Hoffman, amongst others, to try and get the 356 into America. By the end of 1950 he was gravely ill, and died a national hero in January 1951.

In the meantime, in December 1950, a small design and management office was purchased near the Reutter works, and a racing shop was attached with just enough room for two cars and four mechanics. It was at this stage in the proceedings that the company was registered as Dr Ing. h.c. F. Porsche KG.

The Stuttgart concern had a staff of 108 at the time, with planned production of around ten cars per month. In the event, this target was easily doubled, and nearly 300 Porsche 356s were built in the year. The 500th German-built 356 was driven out of the works in March 1951, and just five months later the 1000th 356 left the factory.

By March 1951, 1283cc engines were available, and a 1488cc unit followed in October. Although the 1100 engine continued until the end of 1954, there were fewer sales of the smaller capacity models, especially in America, a market that was already very important to the company.

In September 1952, the 1500 (1488cc Type 527) gave a refined 55bhp. Fitted with the Albert Hirth-designed roller bearing crankshaft and a special cam, however, this was increased to 70bhp and the car became known as the 1500 Super (Type 528). Other important revisions carried out during 1952 included dropping the old two-piece windscreen, although

the distinct V-shape remained until 1955. Stronger bumpers, now moved further away from the body, were also a feature.

The original Porsche factory was supposed to have been handed back in September 1950 but, due to the alert caused by the Korean War, the American authorities held on to it. With no sign of the old factory being returned, another works was built in 1952, next door to Reutter. By November 1952, the first cars were starting to roll out of Werk II.

From November 1953, a roller bearing version of the 1300, called the 1300 Super (Type 589), was made available. Launched at the Paris Salon, this 60bhp unit was to be short-lived, only remaining in production for six months. In fact, all pushrod roller bearing engines would be phased out by the end of 1957.

Dr Ernst Fuhrmann had begun to design the powerful Carrera engine during 1952. In order to keep the physical size of the engine down, he devised an ingenious system that incorporated no less than nine shafts, fourteen bevel gears and two spur gears to operate the dohc per bank arrangement. The beauty in this system lay in the fact that the engine's overall dimensions were little changed from the standard unit. The first engine was up and running in April 1953; it was right virtually from the start, and testing took place in the new Porsche 550 at the Nürburgring in August.

A Carrera engine was installed in one of the works Gmünd coupés, and entered for the 1954 Liège-Rome-Liège Rally, held that particular year in August. Ferry Porsche's theory was that if the engine could endure such a tough event, it could safely be put into a production car. The decision was made easier after Herbert Linge and Helmut Polensky won outright.

In 1954, staff at the factory increased to 493, but only 1934 cars were produced – 44 fewer than the previous year. However, on 15 March 1954, the 5000th German-made Porsche was built (two years later the figure reached 10,000) and exports now accounted for 60% of production.

John von Neumann, Porsche's west coast distributor, was the inspiration behind the Speedster. The Speedster was exactly what Hoffman needed to boost sales Stateside, selling at $2995 in basic form. Based on the Cabriolet, but with minimal equipment (a cheap hood, a low and flimsy windscreen, and detachable side-screens instead of wind-up windows), it was introduced into America in September 1954. In all, a total of 4854 Speedsters were produced (both 356 and 356A types together), and it became the darling of the racing set.

At the 1951 Earls Court Show, a Porsche 356 coupé and a 356 cabriolet were put on display by Connaught Cars Ltd., becoming the first German cars to be shown in England since the end of the war. Before long, AFN Ltd. of Isleworth (the company behind Frazer-Nash) became the agent, with imports starting seriously in 1954. Prices ranged from £1842 to £2378, which was quite expensive when one considers a Jaguar XK120 cost around £1600 at this time, and the choice of even cheaper British sports cars was almost endless.

The 356A was introduced at the Frankfurt Show in September 1955. There were subtle changes to the body, and suspension improvements made the car feel more stable going into corners. The 356s were still being used successfully in rallying, the Liège-Rome-Liège event becoming a Porsche benefit. The racing side of competition was left almost exclusively to the Spyders, although there were class wins on both the Mille Miglia and Targa Florio.

The 1957 Le Mans 24-hour race. A splendid shot of a privately entered 550A Spyder, a car which made its debut on the 1956 Mille Miglia.

The 1582cc engine came along in 1955, and two versions were available: the 1600 and the 1600 Super, giving 60 and 75bhp respectively. The 1300 and 1300 Super continued unchanged in most markets, but had been dropped in America earlier in the year and were phased out completely by the end of 1957. The 1500GS Carrera engine was made available for the new 356A range and, like the other power units, could be specified in the updated coupé, cabriolet or Speedster bodyshells.

The old works was at last handed back to its rightful owner on 1 December 1955. Called Werk I, the management, along with the Design, Experimental and Racing Departments, moved there, as did the Repair Shop.

Towards the end of 1955, three out of every four cars produced by Porsche (which by now employed around 600 people) were exported, the majority of which found their way to America.

The increase in production resulted in fewer changes being made to the cars. Teardrop tail lights replaced the twin round items in March 1957, but by far the biggest changes came when the T-2 body was introduced at the 1957 Frankfurt Show. Following the show, the Carrera became available in two versions – a De Luxe (GS) model with different carburation and an improved heater, and the GT. The 110bhp GT was available only as a Speedster or coupé, and was aimed squarely at competition.

In August 1958, the Speedster was superseded by the Convertible D (the D being added in recognition of the coachbuilder, Drauz of Heilbronn).

With its more serviceable hood, a better windscreen, padded seats and wind-up side windows, it was much more in line with Ferry Porsche's ideals.

Porsche in competition

Based on the original Porsche Number One, the Type 550 made its debut in May 1953 for the Eifelrennen at the Nürburgring. On this occasion the mid-engined car was powered by a 1500 Super unit but, nonetheless, it narrowly beat the Borgwards to take a maiden class victory. It provided the Porsche concern with the foundation stone on which to build a racing legend.

By the end of of 1954, the first of the customer cars were being completed by Wendler of Reutlingen. The Type 547 Carrera engine was used,

A 356B coupé dating from 1960. Note the higher mounting of the bumpers, one of the features that helps distinguish the 356B from its immediate predecessors.

but tuned to bring the power up to over 100bhp. The official designation was 550/1500RS, but Max Hoffman coined the name Spyder, and it was this title that stuck in the mind of the public.

Excellent results at Le Mans, on the Carrera Panamericana, the Mille Miglia (the 1954 event was the international debut of the 550 Spyder with the Carrera engine), the Tour de France Automobile, the Tourist Trophy, and numerous tracks across Europe and America secured the Spyder a place in racing history.

The Wendler-bodied 550A had been introduced in April 1956. Gone was the ladder chassis of the old Spyder, replaced by a lighter but stiffer spaceframe, and it incorporated a low pivot swing axle rear suspension. The 550A gave Porsche its first taste of victory on the Targa Florio, and there were many class wins.

The Type 718 prototype was built up over the winter of 1956/57. Based on the one-off Type 645, it was a lighter machine again, built around a spaceframe chassis and some five inches lower than the old 550 Spyder. Improved suspension, superior braking and 142bhp resulted in a far better car. The mid-engined 718 RS became the 718 RSK through further suspension changes – these later reverted back, but the RSK name stayed.

Formula Two returned in 1957, the new regulations dictating that 1.5 litre engines running on pump fuel would form the basis for the series. Porsche entered a couple of races, and actually won the F2 Class at the Nürburgring Grand Prix with a 550A.

The RSK had made only two appearances at the race track in the 1957 season but, by the early part of 1958, the definitive 718 RSK had arrived. On the 1959 Targa Florio, Edgar Barth and Wolfgang Seidel took Porsche's second victory in the classic event, followed home by three other Porsche drivers.

As early as 1953, Ferry Porsche had hinted that Porsche may become involved in Grand Prix racing. During October 1958, the CSI announced that Formula One would run with 1.5 litre cars with a minimum weight of 500kg for 1961 – the rules seemed ideally suited to Porsche.

In the meantime, the company continued to field the RSK in Formula Two races. A programme was instigated so that Porsche would have an open-wheeled F2 car for 1959, using it as a test-bed for the proposed F1 machine for 1961. It was running by April 1959, and was very much the same as the Type 718 under the skin, save for the new narrow chassis frame and detail changes that this necessitated.

The car was improved as the year progressed. Stirling Moss was impressed enough by the German car to test it, with the result being that Rob Walker was loaned one of the new works F2 cars for Moss' use during the 1960 season. Porsche won the 1960 Formula Two Championship.

The company's F1 debut came at Brussels on 9 April 1961, but it consistently failed to get the desired results. Dan Gurney's victory in the 1962 French Grand Prix was to be Porsche's only win in a World Championship event. Formula One proved too expensive and, despite having invested a small fortune in developing the flat eight engine, Porsche decided to cut its losses and withdraw gracefully from the Grand Prix scene.

To meet the ever-increasing threat from Alfa Romeo and Lotus, Porsche exploited FIA rules to the limit, and had a new Carrera made ready in order to maintain position at the top of the 1600 Class. 25 chassis were reserved by Porsche for the Abarth-Carrera project, although eventually only 20 of the lightweight, Zagato-bodied cars

stronger bumpers. The standard 1.6 litre 60bhp engine of the 356A was retained, as was the Super, but this was now known as the Super 75 to differentiate it from the new Super 90. This 90bhp unit was available from March 1960, and was considered powerful enough to render the Carrera model unnecessary. For the time being at least, there was no Carrera listed.

The 356B was initially catalogued with three body styles. The Convertible D was renamed the Roadster, and the coupé and cabriolet made up the range. In August 1960, they were joined by the short-lived Karmann hardtop coupé. A third factory (Werk III) had been built at Zuffenhausen towards the end of 1959 to cope with the workload, and, by 1960, annual turnover was around 90,000,000 DM!

At the Frankfurt Show in September 1961, the T-6 body made its debut. There were a number of new features to distinguish the latest model, such as the larger front and rear windows on the coupé, a new engine cover with two grilles fitted across the range, and a larger front hood featuring a squarer-shaped leading edge (which, in turn, meant more luggage space).

At the same time as the T-6 356B was introduced, the Carrera returned to the line-up. Named the Carrera 2, it had a two litre version of the Carrera engine, and was sold to the public from the following April. The Carrera 2 introduced disc brakes to the Porsche marque for the first time, and with 130bhp on tap, a top speed of 124mph was possible. The 50,000th German-built Porsche left the line in April 1962,

were built. Four or five were made ready for works drivers in 1960 – class wins came at Le Mans, on the Targa Florio, at Sebring and the Nürburgring.

The RS60 had a larger windscreen than the old RSK to meet new FIA regulations for 1960. Otherwise, the RS60 was basically similar to the 718, except for the slightly longer wheelbase and more powerful engine. The similar-looking RS61 followed for the 1961 season.

356 developments
The 356B made its public debut at the 1959 Frankfurt Show, distinguishable by the higher position of the headlights in a new wing line, and higher and

A 356C 1600SC coupé and its ultimate replacement, the 911. The picture dates from 1964, a time when the two models would have been built and sold alongside each other.

but shortly afterwards the Karmann hardtop coupé and the Roadster were discontinued due to falling sales.

Introduced in July 1963, the 356C was basically a stop-gap model until the new 911 became established. More refined than its predecessors, the body was very much the same as that seen on the 356B (offered in coupé and cabriolet forms, with the option of a detachable steel hardtop for the latter). The main changes were mechanical.

There were new 75 and 95bhp engines, a modified rear suspension, and disc brakes were standard across the range. However, the basic layout of four air-cooled cylinders, horizontally opposed in pairs, remained unchanged throughout the seventeen year lifespan of the 356. The body had changed little, but all the time it was being brought up-to-date, regularly acquiring features tested in the field of motorsport.

Porsche thought that a white cabriolet, completed in September

1965, was going to be the last 356. Officially it was, but then the Dutch Police placed a special order for ten vehicles in 1966 – they were initiated in March. The total number of 356s built came to 76,313.

Despite the demand for the 356, it was obvious that the model was not going to last forever, and Porsche started to prepare for its ultimate replacement in the late-fifties. Ferry Porsche wanted the new car to be slightly bigger and a true 2+2. The Type 695 project began in 1959, but was later rejected in favour of a new coupé design from Butzi Porsche – the Type 901.

The 911 and 912

Butzi (officially Ferdinand Alexander), the eldest of Ferry Porsche's sons, was born in 1935. He had joined Porsche's Styling Department in 1957, taking charge of it four years later. This was not nepotism as Butzi

became a very accomplished designer. Erwin Komenda, who had been with Porsche since its earliest days, did the engineering side of the bodywork.

With the flat four getting close to the end of its development, however, it became necessary to look at a new power unit. The flat four was powerful enough in Carrera guise, but was expensive to build, so, in 1961, design work on a new power unit was initiated.

As time passed by and the Type 901 project came ever closer to becoming a reality, it was decided that the flat eight Grand Prix engine would form the basis for the new unit. Shortened to a six cylinder layout, and using just one overhead camshaft per bank instead of two, the 130bhp two litre engine was also given the Type 901 designation It was developed by Hans Tomala (the former head of the R&D Department), and was ready for testing in the early part of 1962.

The Porsche 901, whilst retaining

A 1968 model year 912. For the following season, there was a completely new four cylinder Porsche.

many of the features of its predecessor, was a completely new car. Although the rear-mounted, air-cooled boxer engine layout was kept, along with the famous Porsche baulk-ring gearbox and all-round independent suspension, it was a larger car. The 901 was first seen at the Frankfurt Show in 1963, but the production cars wouldn't roll off the line at Zuffenhausen until the following year. By that time, the 901 designation was altered to 911 after a complaint from Peugeot regarding the use of "its" numbering system.

The 911 was eventually made available to the public at 21,900 DM from September 1964. Then, in May 1965, Porsche introduced the 912. The body, suspension and braking system were identical to the six cylinder 911, but the 912 was far closer to the 356 in that they shared the same Super 90 power unit, albeit in modified form. Most of the 356s built in 1965 had gone to the States, and the 911 was

produced alongside the 356 in the latter's final years.

The 911 was introduced to the American public at the start of 1965. The 912 was announced in July 1965, going on sale two months later, just as the 356 series officially ran out. The American market remained the most important for Porsche and its pricing policy there was interesting. In its final year, an SC coupé would have cost $4577 in basic form, whilst the 911 was $6490. The 912, however, was just $4690 – about the same as the earlier four cylinder model.

Initially, two versions of the 912 were offered: the 912/4 with four speed transmission, and the 912/5 with a five speed. Whereas the 911 had five gauges on the wood-trimmed fascia, the 912 had only three and no wood. Capable of around 115mph, 0-60 came up in a fraction under 12 seconds – performance was therefore about the same as for the 356C 1600SC coupé.

Perhaps the most important change during the early life of the new car was the availability of the Targa body (announced in September 1965 but not sold until the following year), listed for both the 911 and 912. During 1966 and 1967 respectively, two more variations on the 911 were announced – a 160bhp 911S (capable of 140mph) and the basic 911T. At the same time, Porsche's trademark five-spoke alloy wheels were announced, and a semi-automatic 'Sportomatic' gearbox became an option.

Not surprisingly, with Porsche's policy of constant evolution, a second generation 911 (the B-series) was launched in September 1968, with a longer wheelbase and flared wheelarches covering the wider wheels and tyres. The 911E was introduced at this time, placed in between the T and S. While the T retained its twin Weber carburettors, both of the higher powered machines now featured Bosch

Works driver, Bjorn Waldegaard, hustling the 911S to victory on the 1970 Monte Carlo Rally.

mechanical fuel injection.

In the following year, engine size rose to 2195cc via an increase in the bore, with power outputs now being quoted at 125, 155 and 180bhp respectively for the T, E and S grades (both of the latter models came with fuel injection and a five speed gearbox as standard). This 2.2 litre range was subsequently christened the C-series.

Approximately 30,000 911s were built from 1965 to 1969, along with a similar number of 912s over the same period. The 911 was proving itself an excellent rally car, winning the

17

The 904 GTS Carrera on the 1964 Targa Florio. The elegant body was designed by Butzi Porsche, Ferry's eldest son.

prestigious Monte Carlo Rally in 1968, 1969 and 1970. At the 1969 Frankfurt Show, a new, four cylinder Porsche was introduced for the 1970 season.

A competition update

Ferry Porsche gave the go-ahead for a new, mid-engined competition car at the end of 1962 – the 904. The lightweight glassfibre body (glassfibre was chosen to speed up production since four or five cars had to be built each day if the new model was to homologated for the 1964 season) was bonded to the chassis for extra strength. Records show that well over 100 were built, with most of the works cars having six- or eight-cylinder power units.

The new car's first major race was at Sebring in March 1964, where it ran as a prototype – it was eventually homologated in April. Shortly after, the

The gorgeous Porsche 907 seen on the 1968 Targa Florio. In the following year, the 907 was ultimately superseded by the all-conquering 917 model, giving the German marque its first Le Mans victory in 1970.

904, driven by Colin Davis and Antonio Pucci, won the 1964 Targa Florio, with Linge and Balzarini finishing second. Ultimately, the 904 dominated two litre sports car racing during the 1964 and 1965 seasons.

Ferry Porsche had already approved production of another 100 cars, but then Ferdinand Piech (the son of Ferry's sister, who had joined the company in 1963) took over the Research & Development Department and, therefore, the competition shop. Piech had grander ideas, and from now on Porsche's philosophy on racing changed, with the cars moving further and further away from their road-going counterparts. Piech set the marque down a route of producing pure racers, culminating in the all-conquering 917.

Among numerous outstanding victories, Porsche won the Targa Florio in 1966, 1967, 1968, 1969 and 1970 (all with different drivers), and again in 1973. However, in September 1971, Ernst Fuhrmann returned to the Porsche camp, following a tenure at the Goetze piston ring company, and duly took Piech's place as head of engineering and, as such, the racing team.

It's interesting to note, given the close bond between race and road machines in the 356 era, that Fuhrmann considered the current breed of racing cars too far removed from the road vehicles to be of any real use in marketing. It will be remembered that, not long after his return, a whole range of sporting machinery stemmed from the 911 and, once again, the Porsche road and racing cars were unequivocally linked.

PORSCHE 924

2

THE 914: A JOINT PROJECT

The evergreen VW Beetle and Karmann Ghia (rear and far right). Credit for the Beetle's design lies with the Porsche family – the Volkswagen and Porsche marques have always been unequivocally linked.

The origin of the Volkswagen (or People's Car) is well known: designed by Professor Porsche, the commission came in mid-1934 from Adolf Hitler, leader of the Nazi Party and Germany's Chancellor. Hitler was keen to promote German industry, but his boldest automotive plan by far was to equip every German in the Third Reich with a similar motor car. The vehicle would, of course, become known the world over as the Beetle.

The VW was naturally given state backing, and Porsche was even told to visit the United States to study mass-production methods. However, after just 210 Beetles had

been built in a dedicated factory just outside Hannover, the events of 1939 intervened and soon put an end to the Volkswagen, albeit temporarily.

The British occupying force helped to get the project back on-line following the end of hostilities, and, by 1948, control of the Wolfsburg factory had been handed back to the Germans. An ex-Opel and BMW worker, Heinz Nordhoff, was appointed General Manager and the company thrived. The VW Beetle success story had begun.

The Karmann four-seater cabriolet was introduced in July 1949, by which time Beetle exports were becoming increasingly significant. By 1953, the

*Professor Heinz Nordhoff,
Volkswagen's influential leader, and a
strong Porsche ally.*

factory at Wolfsburg was employing over 20,000 people to make an average of 670 cars a day, seeing off the competition (coming mainly from Auto Union in the shape of the DKW) by consistently cutting prices. In August 1955, the one millionth Beetle was produced – within four years, the figure had reached three million!

The origins of the Karmann coachbuilding business in Osnabrück can be traced back to the 1870s. The Karmann Ghia sports car, styled by Ghia's Luigi Segre, was announced in July 1955. Powered by an almost standard 1.2 litre VW Beetle engine, the new model gained a loyal following, after the 1955 Frankfurt Show, and no less than 1282 were sold by the end of the first year.

All of the modifications and improvements made to the Beetle were carried over to the Karmann Ghia, and a cabriolet version was put on the market in August 1957. By the end of that year, around 15,000 Karmann Ghias had been built in the ever-expanding Osnabrück factory, with almost half of them going to the United States.

Over 23,000 Karmann Ghias had been produced by the end of 1962, by which time the 'Type 3' Karmann Ghia had made its debut. The Type 3 version, with its unique coupé body, was powered by the larger 1.5 litre engine (later enlarged to 1.6 litres in line with the Beetle saloon), but was to be short-lived by Volkswagen standards, continuing until mid-1969 only. However, the original-style models continued to sell strongly. In fact, apart from the running changes brought about by improvements in the Beetle, the Karmann Ghia changed very little during its long history.

VW's links with Porsche

After the signing of the 1948 agreement, Nordhoff had provided the Stuttgart firm with a constant stream of commissions, as well as allowing Porsche access to components, and use of the Volkswagen sales and service network. Indeed, Porsche had dealt with around 60 projects for VW before the 914 model was instigated, ranging from complete cars for the marque, to engines and transmissions, as well as more mundane items such as heating systems.

Early projects – some actually started in Gmünd – included the designs for a complete car that was slightly smaller than the Beetle, and even an electrically-driven machine. One of the most interesting design proposals to come from Porsche was the Type 672 of 1955. This was to be a small car with a rear-mounted, under-floor engine. Tests were carried out with V6 engines of 1.2 and 1.5 litres, but eventually an air-cooled flat six was chosen. The 1.5 litre version produced 54bhp, and was without doubt a view of the future.

Another noteworthy Porsche design for VW was the stillborn Type 700, an early form of people carrier. Then, in March 1958, Porsche, alongside VW's own styling department and Ghia of Italy, was commissioned to design a new bodyshell for a medium-sized car. Porsche came up with several variations powered by an under-floor flat four engine. The Type 728 (or EA-53 in Volkswagen terminology) eventually resulted in the VW Type 3. Meanwhile, Porsche had developed a number of improvements for the Beetle, including the synchromesh gearbox which was adopted from 1951 on this most famous of Volkswagens.

The VW success story

During the 1950s, Volkswagen had established a number of sales

Audi provided another link with the past for Porsche. Audi's origins could be traced back to Auto Union (it even carried the same badge), and its famous V16 Grand Prix car was another Porsche design, of course. Now Audi belonged to Volkswagen.

companies all over the world, including a special arrangement with the Porsche family in Austria, and had even started to set up the first of many overseas production plants. On 22 August 1960, Volkswagenwerk GmbH was formed with a capital of DM 600 million.

In light of increasing competition from Ford and Opel, Nordhoff needed some new products, since it was obvious that VW couldn't rely solely on the Beetle forever. The all-new Type 3, or VW 1500, arrived in May 1961. Like the Variant that followed in 1963, it was available as either a saloon or an estate car.

Auto Union had been bought by Daimler-Benz during 1958/59, but executive control shifted to Wolfsburg in 1964 and Audi AG was formed. At the end of the decade, Volkswagen bought the ailing NSU concern and merged it with Audi in August 1969.

By 1967, Volkswagen, building more than a million cars a year, had quite an extensive range on offer and, in the background, Porsche was developing a replacement for the Beetle. Despite this, however, the German company was replaced by Fiat as the largest car producer in Europe at that time.

A joint project

In view of the vast history shared by Porsche and Volkswagen, it was perhaps inevitable that the two companies should at some stage produce a joint project. That time came in the mid-1960s when each concern was faced with a dilemma.

Volkswagen sales were on the

decline as competition increased from a new breed of economy cars. New models were in hand to cover the sector of the market currently occupied by the Beetle, which, despite this drop in sales, went on to replace the Model T Ford as the most successful car ever made, with production easily passing the 15 million mark in February 1972. The Karmann Ghia, however, was also considered out of date, so a new,

affordable, two-seater sports car was thought necessary.

Porsche was also in need of something new. The price of the 911 had escalated far more than the Stuttgart firm had anticipated, and the cheaper 912 was not selling anywhere near quickly enough to keep the dealers happy, mainly because less expensive, but equally competent, sports cars were coming from a number of other

The NSU marque, renowned for its work on the rotary engine, also became part of the growing VW empire. NSU was duly merged with Audi, and then allowed to fade away. However, the old Neckarsulm factory would later be an important part of the 924 story.

manufacturers.

Following the demise of the 356 range, the 912 had been introduced to offer customers a less complicated and lower-powered version of the 911. Announced in May 1965 (nine months

A prototype built by Giorgetto Giugiaro's ItalDesign as a possible replacement for the Karmann Ghia. Time was running out for the ageing model, and this modern interpretation was displayed at the 1971 Geneva Show. Sadly, it failed to reach production.

The mid-engined 914 was designed to replace the Karmann Ghia and Porsche 912 in one fell swoop. This is an early six cylinder example.

after the 911 launch but well before the last of the 356s were produced), it used a slightly modified Super 90 engine from the outgoing model (designated 616/36), although, except for the equipment level, the rest of the 912 was basically identical to the 911.

When it was introduced, a four speed 912 cost $4690, which was around 72% of the cost of a 911. The body/chassis modifications applied to the 911 series were carried over to the 912 but, by 1968, the price of the four cylinder car was within 12% of the basic six cylinder model; it simply wasn't worth Porsche selling the car any cheaper. With substantially less power on tap, but very little difference in cost, most buyers naturally opted for the 911, and sales of the 912 were very slow.

Porsche needed an entry-level machine that would sell in volume, preferably using a six cylinder engine in the interests of standardisation. However, developing a new model was a costly undertaking and, besides, Porsche had neither the finance nor the production capacity. A joint project with VW was the obvious answer and Ferry Porsche went on record stating that it came about "from the realization that we needed to broaden our programme at a less costly level and that we couldn't do it alone."

At this early stage, whilst talking over the arrangements, Nordhoff agreed that if Porsche designed and helped develop the new sports car, the Stuttgart company could use the bodies to ultimately make two versions: one with a VW engine and badge, and a more powerful model with a Porsche crest on the bonnet and a six cylinder engine. Because VW would be ordering the car in such large quantities, the cost to Porsche would be significantly reduced.

It was the perfect solution for both concerns. Volkswagen (apart from having Porsche's expert input in a field in which it had little experience) would have a replacement for the Karmann Ghia, and Porsche gained access to a much needed high volume seller without having to invest in expensive tooling and development costs.

The 914 is born

Porsche campaigned various mid-engined competition cars over the years but, by the late-1960s, an increasing number of exotic road cars with this layout had emerged. The Lamborghini Miura made its debut in 1966 and, the following year, there was the Ferrari Dino, the Lotus Europa, the Matra M530 and the DeTomaso Mangusta.

It was also quite interesting to note that a number of specialist manufacturers were turning to larger concerns for their engines. Of the serious competitors to the proposed new sports car, the Pininfarina-bodied Ferrari Dino had its V6 engines produced by Fiat, Lotus sourced its engines from Renault, and Matra used the Ford Taunus V4 engine and transmission.

Porsche had known for several decades that the mid-engined concept was ideal for sports cars, the superior weight distribution aiding handling. It was only a matter of time before Porsche adopted this layout for a road car, and VW was more than happy to back the proposal. The possibilities of adapting the 904 for road use had been investigated in the past, but the idea was rejected. In any case, the design for the new sports car had to be far more practical and, as part of the brief, had to look neither too much like a Porsche or a Volkswagen, whilst at the same time being agreeable to both parties.

As it happened, Porsche already knew of a suitable design produced by Gugelot Design GmbH at its offices in Neu-Ulm. Gugelot was actually an industrial design company, but, during the early-1960s, had decided to produce a proposal for an automobile. From 1966, test cars were presented to a number of big German companies, Porsche included. When the joint sports car project was first mooted, the Gugelot design seemed like an ideal starting point.

Although it was a front-engined machine made of advanced composite materials at this stage, it was acquired by Porsche in the autumn of 1966 and converted to mid-engined configuration to accept either a VW or Porsche lump. The new car, designated the Type 914, retained a targa roof and pop-up headlights, but was given fresh styling crafted in more conventional steel panels over a welded pressed steel structure.

The final designs were passed by Volkswagen in 1967. Since Karmann was producing the Karmann Ghia at the time, and had been heavily involved with both companies in the past, it was a natural choice to build the bodies for the new car. It was agreed that the VW model would be completely built, assembled and trimmed in Osnabrück, whilst the six cylinder version would be shipped as a plain bodyshell to Zuffenhausen so that Porsche could assemble and finish the machine on the same line as the 911.

A turning point
Ferry Porsche and Heinz Nordhoff had enjoyed a splendid working relationship for many years, a bond strengthened by the marriage of one of Porsche's nephews to the VW boss's daughter. Nordhoff, however, was due to retire in 1970 and, in preparation, Kurt Lotz was brought in, from an industrial company in Switzerland, as Nordhoff's deputy in June 1967. It was planned that Lotz would gradually take over the reins but, only one month after he had arrived, Nordhoff became seriously ill, giving the newcomer no time at all to learn of Nordhoff's personal arrangements.

On 1 March 1968, the first prototype 914 (a four cylinder model) was driven, but then, on 12 April, Professor Heinz Nordhoff died. Not only was this a great blow to Volkswagen and all those who knew him, it would also cause immense problems for Ferry

Porsche regarding the 914 project. The problem was that Nordhoff and Porsche had only a 'gentleman's agreement' for the supply of 914 bodies from Karmann. This was nothing unusual, as the two men often worked on a verbal deal basis. However, the new man at Wolfsburg, quite naturally, wanted to see something in writing.

Lotz considered that VW had exclusive rights to the 914 design. Ferry Porsche was told that if he wanted 914 bodies, he would have to buy them at a price which accounted for a percentage of the tooling costs, naturally making them much more expensive. The whole episode could so easily have ended in deadlock but, fortunately, a deal was struck that would ultimately suit both parties.

Eventually, after much negotiation, an agreement was reached whereby Porsche and Volkswagen would form a separate company, both partners having a 50% holding. The plan was announced in January 1969 and, in the following April, VW-Porsche Vertriebsgesellschaft GmbH (or VG for short) was established in Stuttgart with a working capital of DM 5 million.

This new concern would be responsible for marketing and distributing the VW-Porsche 914 series and the 911 in most markets, with the notable exception of America, which would have a completely separate sales organisation. One Managing Director was appointed from VW, Klaus Schneider, while the other, Otto Filius, came from Porsche. Huschke von Hanstein, Porsche's old racing

team manager, was given the job of handling the VG's publicity.

Although setting up a new concern seemed a rather dramatic move, it was, in effect, little more than making a previous arrangement official – Porsche cars had been distributed through VW outlets anyway, except in Britain and France. Nonetheless, the announcement sent rumours around the globe about a possible merger until they were quashed by a blunt press release from Stuttgart.

Lotz, in the meantime, had brought in a new boss for VW's R&D section, though Porsche was still asked to develop the successor to the Beetle (EA-266, or Type 1966 within Porsche), along with Audi and NSU. The latter soon fell by the wayside, leaving just Porsche and Audi working on the project.

Porsche came up with a number of mid-engined designs, including a four-seater saloon, a two-seater version and a 2+2 coupé. The power plant was to be a four cylinder, water-cooled unit of between 800cc and 1.8 litres, developing up to 105bhp for the larger capacity engine. However, after much development work under the supervision of Ferdinand Piech (said to have cost up to DM 250 million), the whole programme was eventually cancelled in the early-1970s as the vehicles would simply have been too costly to produce.

The 914 in detail
There were to be two different models. The Volkswagen version, the 914/4, would be powered by the 1679cc, air-

cooled, flat four engine from the 411E model, using VW's new electronic injection system, allowing it to meet all American emission requirements (including those for California).

It was expected that around three quarters of the 914s produced would be fitted with the four cylinder Volkswagen engine. Many Porsche fans were enraged by this but, as Road Test magazine pointed out: "Although the concept of a VW engine in what is obviously intended to be a spirited performing GT machine might raise a few eyebrows, the current 411 engine is nearly on a performance par with the Super 90 or 912 engine, which was at the top of the four cylinder Porsche engine line."

The VW 411 had been introduced in August 1968, with the fuel-injected 411E following a year later. There was little doubt that the advanced VW engine was a highly respected unit within the industry, and it's mid-mounting endowed the 914 with excellent weight distribution, said to be some 10% better than that of the contemporary 911.

The Porsche model, known as the 914/6, would be equipped with the classic six cylinder, air-cooled engine from the 1969 model year 911T, rated at 110bhp – 30bhp more than the VW unit installed in the 914/4. As a matter of interest, there were three 911 engine options available at that time: the 911T, the 140bhp 911E and the top-of-the-range 170bhp 911S.

The definitive flat six Porsche engine appeared in autumn 1963. Overseen by Hans Tomala, and

known as the Type 901, it was a 1991cc, all alloy, air-cooled unit with a single overhead chain driven camshaft per bank. Originally, three single-choke downdraught Solex carburettors were used on each bank, replaced by triple-choke Webers from the beginning of 1966. To overcome oil surge during hard cornering, the 130bhp power unit was given dry sump lubrication.

Incidentally, the 1969 model year engine was chosen for the 914/6 as this kept the new model at two litres. The 911 range had been given 2.2 litre engines (available in three states of tune) for the 1970 model year, and introduced alongside the new 914/4 and 914/6 in September 1969.

A five speed gearbox was offered in both versions to give effortless high speed cruising, although the ratios were altered to suit the torque of the different engines. Suspension was via MacPherson struts, lower wishbones and longitudinal torsion bars at the front, with semi-trailing arms and coil springs to the rear in order to make room for the engine. The spring rates were very hard, eliminating the need for anti-roll bars on the standard road cars. Despite this, Porsche's tests recorded higher cornering powers for the 914 than for the contemporary 911. Disc brakes were employed on all four wheels and, like the steering components, came from either the Porsche or VW parts bin, depending on the power plant. Both models had the handbrake situated between the driver's seat and the sill to allow for an optional third 'seat'.

Launch of the new model
After the 1969 Frankfurt Show, the four cylinder model was available almost immediately, while its six cylinder stablemate was to be available from the following February. Initial production schedules called for a total of 30,000 cars a year, the 1.7 litre four cylinder car commencing in October 1969, while 914/6 production was due to start at the end of the year, replacing the 912 in the Porsche range.

Part of the agreement with Volkswagen stipulated that the 914 range would be badged as VW-Porsche, naturally adding kudos to the four cylinder model. The only exception to this rule was in America, where all models would be called Porsches, regardless of the power unit. Of course, the United States was going to be the most important market (the US took 46% of Porsche production in 1969), and this ploy tied in perfectly with the newly-formed Porsche+Audi sales organisation based in New Jersey.

In the June 1970 issue of Motor Trend, the situation in the USA was explained as follows:

"Last year Porsche entered into a marketing/engineering agreement with Volkswagen who had just bought control of Audi-NSU. Porsche would enjoy VW's worldwide organization to disburse their finely crafted sports cars and VW would have access to Porsche's super engineering staff for development/prototype work. More than that, Porsche would equip its 914s mostly with VW engines – the power plant Wolfsburg created for their 411 model.

"In the US, Volkswagen of America, which is still the funnel through which all VW-Porsche products flow, decided that it was best to now separate the familiar old VW-Porsche dealer. The VW is an economy car and they want it left that way. The Porsche is an expensive (in comparison) sports car and should rightly have its own place in the sun. So VW of America went to their VW-Porsche dealers and said they would have to decide for VW or Porsche or split their dealership in two and have one location for VW, one for Porsche. No more of this under-the-same-roof-stuff. To make life easier for the Porsche man, he was given the Audi, making him a Porsche-Audi man.

"Last October 1, Porsche-Audi made the paper switch from VW and on November 1 began establishing new dealers, worrying about delivery routes and dates, wondering where they would keep all those spare parts.

"Before the VW-Porsche tie-in, Porsches weren't shipped with VWs, often leaving the Porsches in something less than concours condition. Now they're all shipped together to various unloading points around the country and shipped inland by car carrier. Then it's on to the dealer.

"You really have to admire Porsche and VW, not just for their cars, but their thinking. In the early-1960s the cost of a Porsche, be it the Normal or Super 90 model, ranged in the area of $4000 to $5000. Up until the 914s, the only Porsches available were the $6000 and dearer 911 series. Now they've taken us back to the early-60s, cost wise, and have not only saved us money,

but offered a faster, better handling car that's just as revolutionary as the Porsche Normal of the early-60s."

However, behind the scenes, there were problems with the new system. Before the 914 went on sale in America, the number of authorised Porsche retail outlets fell by one third, the reason being that any dealer wishing to retain the Porsche franchise had to invest around $250,000 in a separate facility. It was hardly surprising, therefore, that many dealers decided the outlay simply couldn't be justified.

The situation for Porsche was not helped by the fact that, as part of the agreement regarding the 914, bodies were only supplied by Karmann fully painted and trimmed, adding to the cost. Furthermore, as mentioned earlier, they were already costing Porsche far more than was first anticipated: actually, they were dearer than the more complicated 911 bodyshells. As a result, the price of the six cylinder 914 would not be all that different from that of the 911, which reduced its worth somewhat in the Porsche line-up.

By 1970, Porsche was producing around 70 cars a day, taking the annual total to 16,757. Now capitalised at DM 20 million, the factory employed around 4000 people. By far the most important market for the Stuttgart firm was America, but the majority of the press was very slow to warm to the new VW-engined model. On the other hand, *Motor Trend* voted the 914 range as 1970 'Import Car of the Year', stating: "Some think it ugly, underpowered, overpriced. Critics have even accused it

of not being a real Porsche ... Whatever the car is or is not, there is a consensus on one point, the 914 is a thoroughly modern automobile."

The four cylinder 914 initially sold for $3695 on the American west coast, which was $100 more than the east coast Port of Entry (POE) price. On the west coast the 914/6 would have cost $6099 and the 911T Targa $7205 during the same period. Interestingly, the latter was only $6235 in the previous year.

In the UK, the guide to the 1969 Earls Court Show stated: "History comes full circle with the introduction of cars combining elements of the exotic Porsche and the homely Volkswagen." It should be noted that the UK had only the 914S specification four cylinder cars, and the first 914/6 didn't arrive there until May. In UK trim, the £3475 914/6 was capable of covering 0-60mph in 8.8 seconds before going on to a top speed of 120mph.

Autocar thought the 914/6 an "expensive but practical mid-engined coupé." The Targa top was a good compromise for the English weather, performance was excellent, and fuel economy quite good. The engine was "rather noisy at town speeds" and the gearchange "tricky". However, stability and handling characteristics were singled out as being outstanding.

Right-hand drive 914s were not produced by the factory, as the Volkswagen element of the partnership was anxious to retrieve tooling costs as quickly as possible. However, a company did offer rhd conversions, although very few people opted to

Jo Siffert and Brian Redman won the 1970 Targa Florio in this lightweight 908/3. It gave an excellent opportunity to preach about the advantages of a mid-engined car.

make an already expensive car even more costly.

Progress of the 914

The German price list from November 1970 had the standard 914/4 at DM 11,955, whilst the same model with the popular S-pack option cost just DM 745 more. The standard six cylinder 914/6 was quoted at a hefty DM 19,980.

However, the stronger economy in Germany led in turn to a weaker dollar, making Porsches very expensive in the US. The value of the deutschmark had risen steadily against the dollar after the 914 was launched, but this not only made imported cars more expensive, if a price was retained in America, it also

gave less return for the manufacturer in dollar sales.

In fact, by the close of 1970, VW-Porsche's financial results were so bad that it seriously considered abandoning the entire 914 project. After all, a loss of DM 200 million is not something to be taken lightly!

Despite reservations, the 914 was continued and, for the 1971 model year, there were several minor changes. Slightly later, in May 1971, Porsche launched the M471 body/wheel package, which gave 914/6 owners the chance to own a GT lookalike – it was not offered for the 914/4. The option included steel wheelarch extensions to cover the 6J x 15 forged Fuchs alloy

wheels, new fibreglass sills to blend in with the flared arches, and a front spoiler to match.

The 914 was reported to be selling better in the USA than the 912 had the previous year, but it was not living up to expectations – price seemed to be the 914's biggest problem. For 1972, there were a number of detail improvements, along with some modifications to comply with the latest exhaust emission laws. The latter problem was dealt with via the four cylinder EA80 engine, which replaced the previous W80 unit; the flat six continued unchanged. In the meantime, the standard 911 range for 1972 had received another engine size

Porsche did all it could to give the 914 a glamorous image, but it quickly became obvious that, from a sales point of view at least, the 914 series was not going to live up to expectations.

Luggage space was provided in the front and rear of the 914. The targa top was very light, but, when not in use, had to be moved to allow access to the rear compartment.

A four cylinder 914 with optional S-pack in the South of France.

increase, this time to 2341cc, with three power ratings: 130, 165 and 190bhp.

Porsche had already secured approval in the States for the 914/6s to be fitted with 2.4 litre engines for the 1972 model year. Sadly, the idea was not followed through when it was realised that the six cylinder model was getting very close to the end of its short-lived production run.

In 1972, the price of the 914/4 stood at $3755. Early that year, the exchange rate stood at DM 3.2 to the dollar – it had been DM 4 in late-1969. Not raising the price of the 914 range much meant less profit for VW-Porsche and, as a result, the 914/6 became a special order vehicle in the States. At the same time, a 911T Targa was $7985 ($735 more than the coupé), and the top model, the 911S Targa, was priced at $10,230.

Corporate matters

Denis Jenkinson, with his ear always close to the ground, wrote the following for *Motor Sport* in July 1972:

"Since 1962, Porsche have been quietly, but steadily, building up a private research centre some miles west of Stuttgart near the small village of Weissach. It has taken 10 years, three and a half of them very concentrated, and something like the investment of £8,000,000 in order to complete this very thorough and all-embracing Research and Development Centre, which can tackle the design, building, developing and testing of anything to do with engineering. The growth of the Weissach centre was concurrent with the all-out onslaught that Porsche made on sports car racing, culminating in the World Manufacturers' Championship for the legendary 917 Porsches, and the growth of the testing facilities was speeded up by the racing programme.

"In the management of the Porsche empire there have been some changes made, and Dr. Ferry Porsche and his sister, Louise Piech, and their families still own Porsche, but their sole interest now is in long-term business planning and adjustment of their investments. Since March 1972, control of the engineering has been taken over by Dr. Ing. Ernst Fuhrmann and the business and finance administration by Dipl. Kfm. Heinz Branitzki, these two men now being fully responsible for the future of Porsche. Fuhrmann worked at Porsche as a designer from 1947-1956 and then went to the Goetze Werke engineering firm until he returned to Porsche in 1971, and Branitzki was at Carl Zeiss before joining Porsche in 1965."

On 1 March 1972, the Porsche company was reorganized, with all members of the Porsche family withdrawing. Three companies – Dr. Ing. h.c. F. Porsche KG in Zuffenhausen, the VW-Porsche VG in Ludwigsburg, and the Porsche Konstruktion KG in Salzburg, came under the control of

a holding company, Porsche GmbH, registered in Stuttgart.

Ferry Porsche and Louise Piech were Managing Directors, with Ernst Fuhrmann being responsible for engineering, and Heinz Branitzki was appointed Finance Director. The Sales Director was L. Schmidt, the Development Manager H. Bott, and H. Kurtz was head of production.

Reorganization was completed when Porsche became a joint-stock company, Dr. Ing. h.c. F. Porsche AG. After the family split, Butzi Porsche formed Porsche Design – a highly successful consultancy. Ferdinand Piech went to VW-Audi and helped develop Audi's 4wd system, leading to the world-beating Audi Quattro. Before long he was head of the German company ...

In the meantime, important events were taking place at Volkswagen. Lotz resigned in September 1971, with Rudolf Leiding (a proper VW man) taking his place. Volkswagen had once again lost money in 1971 and, in 1972, Opel overtook VW as the leading German manufacturer in terms of output. However, some consolation was taken from the fact that the 914 became Germany's best-selling sports car, taking the title from the Opel GT.

Leiding was a production specialist, and it was obvious that he supported the new direction brought about by the K70. Originally an Audi-NSU prototype, it catapulted VW into the world of front-wheel-drive, water-cooled machines. Introduced as the VW K70 in 1971, it spelt the end of the NSU marque, and one had to wonder about the future of an air-cooled, mid-engined vehicle ...

914 developments

Initial sales of the 914/6 had seemed promising, but demand quickly tailed off. In the first year of production 2657 cars were built – well below expectations of around 6000 sales worldwide. It became obvious during the second year that the six cylinder machine was not going to sell, and production was cut back dramatically for the 1972 model year. Indeed, only 229 cars were constructed.

Plans to introduce a bigger engined, six cylinder model at the 1971 Paris Salon were duly shelved – the stillborn 916 remaining nothing more than a series of promising prototypes. The 914/6 didn't appear in the 1973 model year line-up, and total production for the type amounted to just 3318 units.

With no 914/6, there was a new four cylinder, two litre model introduced to take its place. To meet ever-stricter emissions regulations in the USA, there was a new 1.7 litre unit for the American market. There was also a new transmission to answer some of the criticism levelled at the old one.

The two litre power unit was basically an enlarged version of the existing flat four. The new capacity was 1971cc – this added up to 100bhp and 115lbft of torque in European trim, enough to take the car from 0-60 in 9.1 seconds, and on to a top speed of 116mph. Engines destined for America had slightly less power and torque due to a lower compression ratio. However, both engines retained the Bosch D-Jetronic fuel injection and a number of other features from the original unit.

To fall into line with the latest regulations, American specification 1.7 litre engines were modified, with the compression ratio dropping from 8.2:1 to just 7.3:1. Naturally, this reduced maximum power, now quoted at 72bhp, and torque output also suffered, being 90lbft on the new EB engine compared to 99lbft on the old EA unit.

The standard 914-1.7 was $4499, whilst the two litre 914S cost $5049. At the same time, a 911T Targa would have cost $8760. The 914S tag was soon dropped – Porsche didn't like the S designation being used – and the official 914-2.0 name was adopted by Porsche+Audi. Nevertheless, it should be noted that the concessionaires in Britain and Australia called the 914-2.0 the 914SC, a title that, strangely, was allowed to continue.

Thanks to the new two litre 914 and the general improvements made to the range, the 1973 model year was to be the 914's most successful sales period, with annual production finishing just 10% short of the original target of 30,000 units a year. With most

A 1973 model year 914 with Fuchs alloy wheels. This is the two litre model, powered by a modified VW flat four unit. Note the pop-up headlights.

of the production going to America, this was no mean feat, as the exchange rate was now less than DM 2.5 to the dollar.

The Volkswagen Type 412 had been introduced for the 1973 model year. It was available as either a two- or four-door saloon, or as an estate car, and initially retained the engine of the 411 (Type 4). The 412 power unit went to 1795cc for 1974, in the heavier four-door and estate models, and it was also used in the Transporter

light commercial series. For 1974, the same engine replaced the 1.7 litre lump for the 914 series as well.

There were two versions, one for America and one for other markets. The American engine, with Bosch L-Jetronic fuel injection, sadly, was suffocated by Federal exhaust emission regulations. Introduced slightly later than the European specification unit in November 1973, it produced just 76bhp at 4800rpm – less power than the original 1.7 litre engine had, despite a larger capacity and bigger valves – and torque was also down. For Europe, the VG decided to produce the 1.8 litre unit equipped with two twin-choke Webers running on a far higher 8.6:1 compression ratio. This added up to a far more lively 85bhp and 105lbft of torque.

The 914 in competition

Porsche had a reputation to uphold. It had won the Manufacturers' Championship in 1969 and, in May of that year, built 25 cars known as the Type 917. The 917's first victory came in a relatively minor race at Zeltweg towards the end of 1969, but a revised version, called the 917K, arrived in time for the 1970 Daytona 24-hour race. There was no looking back – the car totally dominated the racing scene for the next four years.

In a bid to promote the 914 series, the decision was taken to develop the machine for competition. The 914/6 GT was homologated in the FIA's Group 4 on 1 March 1970, after the minimum 500 standard 914/6s had been completed. A total of 12 works

cars were built in Zuffenhausen's Competition Department.

The Nürburgring 1000km Race, held on 31 May 1970, was the international debut of the 914/6 GT. The four cars managed to secure second, third, fourth and fifth in the two litre GT Class, but this achievement was hardly reported, the glory naturally going to the outright win of the 908/03 driven by Elford and Ahrens.

At Le Mans in 1970, the Porsche marque dominated the legendary 24 hour race to take the first of many overall victories at the Sarthe circuit. Porsche veteran Hans Herrmann and Britain's Richard Attwood took their Austrian-entered 917K to victory, followed home by two other Porsches. The excellent performance of Guy Chasseuil and Claude Ballot-Lena was again somewhat overshadowed,

The 914/6 GT entered by Sonauto for the 1970 Le Mans race. Chasseuil and Ballot-Lena came in sixth overall, and took Grand Touring Class honours.

but their win in the Grand Touring category was a significant result for the lone 914/6 model, not least because this equated to sixth overall.

The Marathon de la Route at the Nürburgring was a Porsche 914/6 benefit. Run in August over no less than 84 hours, the three works-entered 914/6 GTs were to be driven by team leaders Gerard Larrousse, Claude Ballot-Lena and Bjorn Waldegaard respectively. The orange-red 914/6 GTs finished first, second and third. A one-two class win at the Österreichring in October gave Porsche some more valuable points in the GT Championship – the first 914/6 GT home secured by a comfortable margin the 1970 International GT Trophy for the Stuttgart marque.

The 914/6 made its official works rally debut on the 1971 Monte Carlo Rally, although a single entry on the 1970 RAC Rally served as a trial run for the most prestigious event on the rallying calendar. Using the same drivers that had brought the Stuttgart firm first, second and fourth places on the 1970 Monte – Bjorn Waldegaard, Gerard Larrousse and Ake Andersson – Porsche prepared three new 914/6s for the 1971 event. Waldegaard finished first in class and a highly respectable joint third overall, although the staff at Porsche had hoped for an even better result to help boost sales. This was to be the last works appearance of the 914 in rallying.

The International Motor Sports Association Championship had just been established in America. It had four general classes, and the one which interested Porsche was the GTU (Gran Turismo, Under 2.5 litres) category in the case of the 914/6 model. With the support of Porsche+Audi, Peter Gregg's 914/6 GT claimed outright victory at three of the IMSA races, and Class wins in the remaining three – enough to take the 1971 IMSA GTU Championship.

Porsche took the flag once again at Le Mans, with the 917K, thanks to Helmut Marko and Gijs van Lennep, repeating the overall success of the previous year. However, the two 914/6s entered fared less well, with both retiring. This was to be the last appearance of the 914 model at the famous Sarthe track. By the end of the year, the 914/6 GT had once again clocked up a vast number of class wins in Europe and America.

However, apart from the occasional class win in minor events, and appearances in SCCA events, the 914 series was being seen less and less. The 914 had come 13th overall and second in class in the 1971 Targa Florio and, in the following year's event, took a class win (ninth overall) courtesy of Schmid and Floridia.

Appropriately, in 1973, Porsche won the final running of the Targa Florio; not with one of the all-conquering sports racers, but a works

Finish of the 1970 Marathon de la Route, with the three works 914/6 GTs at the head of the field. Gerard Larrousse led the Porsches home, boosting the image of the 914 along the way.

The mighty 917K of Helmut Marko and Gijs van Lennep on its way to victory at Le Mans in 1971; it was followed home by another 917, and then its great Ferrari rival, the 512M. The Stuttgart marque had taken the spoils in 1970 with a similar model.

911 Carrera RS driven by Herbert Muller and Gijs van Lennep. In the background there was also a fairly standard 914 wearing number 127 but, unfortunately, it stayed very much in the background and didn't figure in the final placings.

As a matter of interest, it should be noted that Porsche failed to contest the 1972 World Championship because the new regulations – which introduced a three litre engine capacity limit – didn't suit the Stuttgart firm. Instead, Porsche turned its attention to the Can-Am series, the works cars proudly

displaying the Porsche and Audi names side-by-side on the coachwork. Porsche won the series easily in 1972, and then repeated this success the following year.

With the 917 now producing over 1000bhp, Porsche had claimed no less than eight overall victories in the Can-Am series, to take another well deserved title in America. However, for 1974, the rules changed again and the Stuttgart marque stayed away.

Matters of the moment

When the new generation of 911s

with impact bumpers was launched in September 1973, it was noted that engine sizes had been increased again, this time to 2.7 litres for the mainstream cars, with three litres for the top models. This took them even further away from the 914 series in terms of performance and refinement.

In America, the 1.8 litre 914 was $5400–$650 less than the two litre (for comparison, the basic 911 was $9950 at this time, whilst the Targa-bodied version was priced at $10,800). With a poor exchange rate for sales in the USA on such a relatively low-priced

Herbert Muller and Gijs van Lennep campaigned this 911 Carrera RS to win the 1973 Targa Florio. Porsche would gradually return to a policy of racing models based on production cars.

specials on the 914 (including a pair of eight cylinder models) were announced, but sales still fell. In America, the subject of pricing again raised its ugly head. In the July 1974 edition of Road Test magazine it was noted: "The 914 was branded 'overpriced' when it was $2000-$3000 cheaper than it is now, which supposedly elevates it into the outrageously overpriced category, and the 911, which costs about twice as much, into the scandalously overpriced bracket."

There was nothing that could be done – after all, the exchange rates dictated the price, and the Porsche range was barely in line with them. Fortunately, Helmut Schmidt, as Germany's new Chancellor, would bring a modicum of stability in the future.

Company news

In 1974, VW had had to cut back the workforce, despite the launch of the new Passat (known as the Dasher in the USA). New generation water-cooled cars (and the Audi range) eventually pulled the company out of trouble, but, for a moment, there was a serious danger that the business may have failed and had to close its doors.

By July 1974, when Karmann Ghia production ceased, over 360,000 coupés and more than 80,000 cabriolets had been built. It was replaced by an altogether more modern vehicle – the Giugiaro-styled Volkswagen Scirocco, which entered production at the Karmann works during spring 1974.

The 412 was scheduled to be

car, rather against the grain, there were a number of cost-cutting measures introduced for the American market to ensure at least some profit on the cars: the US option list was now as extensive as the European ones.

The only saving grace for the 914 series was that its main competitor, the Opel GT (introduced in September 1968), had been taken out of production. The Matra M530 had also been killed off when Simca-Chrysler took over the Matra concern. Despite an excellent race pedigree, very few were built as, like the 914/6, it had been launched at a far higher price than anticipated.

A number of limited editions and

37

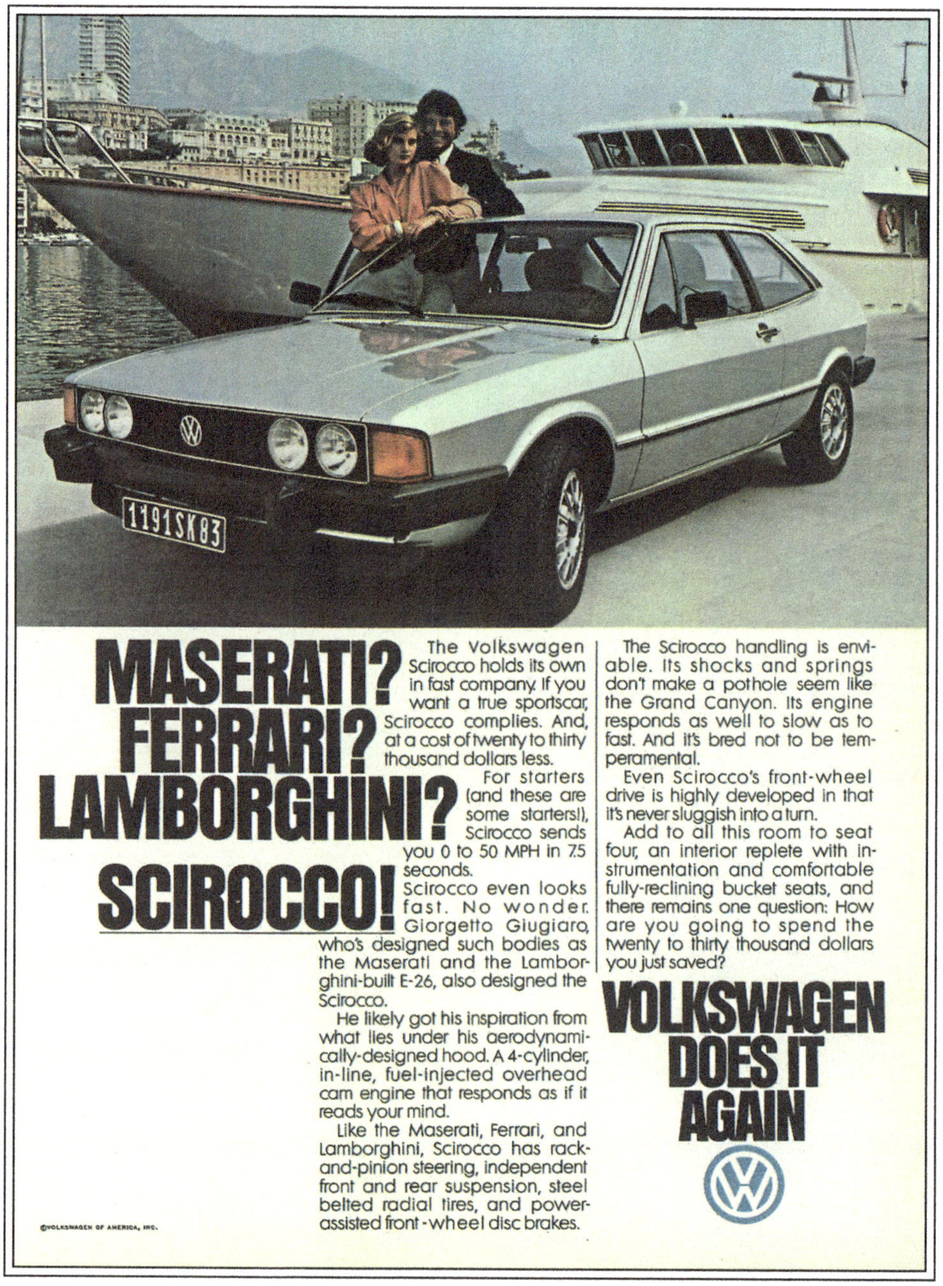

Giorgetto Giugiaro created the lines for Volkswagen's new sporting model, the Scirocco. With the success of the Scirocco, the oil crisis and the ensuing financial climate, the VW management decided not to go ahead with a number of projects, including EA-425 – a significant 2+2 sports coupé. This advert dates from 1979, incidentally.

deleted for 1975. The Passat, Scirocco and Golf all used transverse, water-cooled, in-line fours of 1471cc, although the Scirocco was soon given a 1.6 litre engine to uphold its sporty image.

As Ferry Porsche stated in his fascinating book, *Cars Are My Life*, "This complete change of policy by VW naturally called into question the existence of the joint distribution company, the break-up of which had already been recommended by members of the VW supervisory board. Finally, on 8 May 1974, an agreement to that effect was signed. We acquired VW's stake and moved our sales department into the VG building in Ludwigsburg."

The agreement was retroactive to 1 January 1974, and it brought to an end a very uneasy partnership in which both parties seemed to be pulling in opposite directions. Full control of the 914 shifted to Porsche, although a clause in the agreement ensured that, from the outside, it would seem as though nothing had changed. Interestingly, a number of development contracts were cancelled, although Volkswagen and Porsche did not entirely forsake their long-running alliance.

End of the line

Changes to the 914 for 1975 were headed by a different bumper design. These so-called "crash bumpers" were introduced to comply with the latest US regulations, and actually improved the looks of the car by quite some margin.

A modified two litre engine had to be introduced for the States to satisfy even stricter emissions regulations. It retained the Bosch D-Jetronic fuel injection and virtually the same specification, but the latest emissions equipment drained the power further. Maximum power was now just 88bhp and torque was reduced to 105lbft – figures only just above those quoted for the original 1.7 litre engine.

The 1.8 litre unit was largely unchanged, but a new exhaust system meant there was less torque available (89lbft instead of 94). In California, a catalytic converter and extra anti-pollution equipment was fitted on both engines, making them costlier to produce.

In Germany, the price was held on standard models, but, in America,

A 1975 Porsche 911 Carrera, powered by a 2.7 litre version of the company's legendary flat six engine. This was the year in which the 260bhp 911 Turbo made its debut, having been introduced at the 1974 Paris Salon.

For the 1975 model year, the 914 series bumpers were changed to this new design. The model's days were numbered, however, and Porsche even reintroduced the 912 (the 912E) for the American market for part of the 1976 season. Fortunately, plans were afoot for a more suitable replacement.

the exchange rate and additional costs involved in meeting the emission regulations pushed even the basic 914-1.8 to $6300. Add the options to this, and it became a very expensive car.

Markets were either shrinking, disappearing, or becoming increasingly difficult to satisfy legally. Because of this, the decision was taken to run production down to an absolute minimum, and to sell the 914 series only in America for 1976 – it was about the only country where any sort of demand existed, at least at a level where a profit could be seen. The two litre 914 was priced at $7250 against $10,845 for the 912E – a revamp on the old 912 theme. While the latter could hardly be classed as cheap, it should be borne in mind that the 911S coupé was $13,845 at the time, and the Targa-bodied version was no less than $14,795.

On 10 February 1975, Toni Schmucker, who had spent 33 years with Ford Germany, took over from Rudolf Leiding at Volkswagen. Carrying on from where Leiding left off, the 1795cc VW engine was stopped for the 1976 model year in the VW range when the Transporter series (the only vehicle other than the 914 to still use it) went to two litres, using basically the same engine as found in the 914. For this reason, only the 914-2.0 was offered for 1976.

The last cars were completed in the Osnabrück works during the early part of 1976, with final sales occurring during the spring. There was no announcement; the 914 was simply allowed to fade away.

The VW-Porsche 914 series has often been regarded as a disaster for Porsche and Volkswagen, but this can only be considered true if it is viewed purely in VW production terms, or financial gain. It should be remembered that the entire Porsche 356 run totalled less than 76,500 units, whilst 914 production, at nearly 120,000 units, easily outstripped the mid-engined output from Matra, Lotus and Lancia combined.

The respected author, L.J.K. Setright, put forward his point of view concerning the fate of the 914 in an article in *Classic Cars*. He stated: "Profiteering by the dealers and snobbishness among customers killed the 914/6 – yet it was the only Porsche honestly to make available to the public the features that had gained the marque a phenomenal reputation in racing; and it was upon that reputation that the fortunes of the firm were built in modern times."

Whichever way one looks at the 914, it had a short production history by Porsche and Volkswagen standards. Officially announced in November of 1975, its ultimate replacement, the 924, would also have to face a baptism of fire.

3

THE 924: A NEW TYPE OF PORSCHE

In chapters one and two I hope I've been able to demonstrate that the Porsche and Volkswagen marques have been closely linked since their formative days. They took different routes after establishment, but fundamentally they relied on each other, and their paths crossed many times in the ensuing years.

Sadly, all too often journalists and historians, in one or two lines, dismiss the 924 as nothing more than a VW-Audi kit car with a Porsche badge: if this is the case, then wasn't the 914 range also, not to mention the highly-prized early 356s? As for the lack of an air-cooled engine, it's called progress: is the current 911 or Boxster any less of a Porsche because of it? The previous chapter tells how, in marketing terms, the two companies were perhaps a lot closer than most realize – or, more accurately in many cases, want to acknowledge.

The reality is that the 924 was a Porsche design, developed by Porsche for an outside concern. If the management at Stuttgart wasn't happy with it, there's no way it would have paid out a small fortune to buy back the project.

After all, when Leiding cancelled EA-266 shortly after his appointment as VW's new head, even though Porsche engineers had spent five years developing it, and most of the tooling had been produced (it was in an advanced state, but didn't readily lend itself to interchangeability with other proposed Volkswagen models, thus increasing production costs), Porsche left well alone. This worthy project is conclusive proof that Porsche was hardly in the habit of building something that wouldn't fit in with future plans and the rest of the line.

Furthermore, given declining sales and the world economy at the time, in reality, Porsche needed a competitive entry-level model to keep it afloat; it's very doubtful whether it could have survived purely on 911 buyers, and the upcoming V8 executive express was even more extravagant in an age of escalating fuel prices and an unusually strong deutschmark. Porsche needed the 924.

The situation in 1975

After Nordhoff's death, the relationship between Porsche and Volkswagen became increasingly strained. A lot of the problem was political, but, whatever the reason, the two companies slowly but surely drifted apart. Porsche had a more pressing concern, however, as Dr Fuhrmann predicted the end of the air-cooled engine due to ever-stricter emissions and noise regulations.

With the collapse of the VG, and the 914 on its last legs, this left Porsche with only the 911 to sell; an air-cooled machine with a relatively noisy, all-alloy, high-revving engine and exhaust system located in one area at the back of the vehicle – not an ideal scenario with tighter noise restrictions being introduced, particularly in Germany.

A slower-revving, front-mounted, water-cooled engine started to look attractive, as the water jackets absorb quite a lot of noise, and the bark of the exhaust could be carried the full length of the car, making it easier to pass fixed-

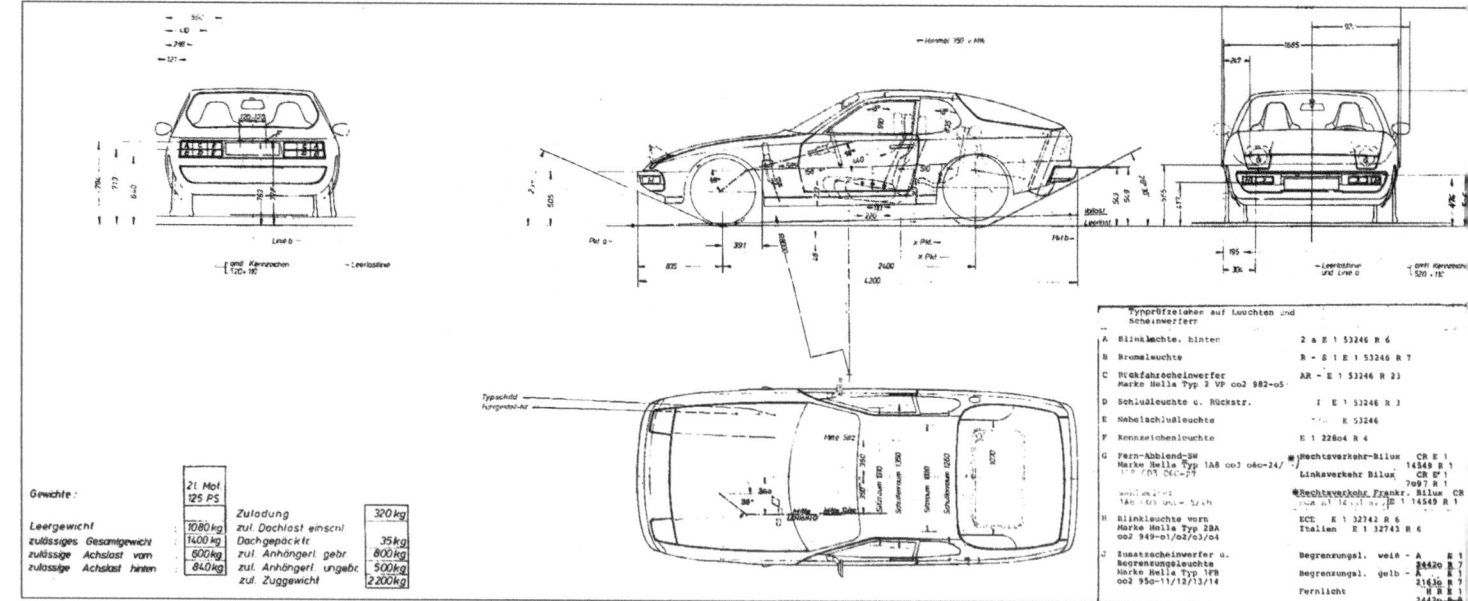

Technical drawing for EA-425, later known as the Porsche 924.

position microphone spot checks. It was also reasoned that a front-mounted engine would allow more space to fit exhaust emission control devices (the much-publicized US regulations for 1975 and '76 were particularly strict, and those originally proposed for 1978 were, frankly, ridiculous), and – an increasingly important factor – make it easier to comply with Federal forward-impact crash tests.

From 1971 there were plans for a front-engined, water-cooled, luxury 2+2 (with a larger cubic capacity to maintain power levels), but it would be some time before this entered production. The suggested price was far too high to give the company enough turnover to survive with any degree of comfort. Perceived originally as a replacement for the 911 (it was envisaged the 911 wouldn't last beyond 1980), this would later be christened the 928.

Porsche, therefore, still required a cheaper entry-level model. As it happened, the Stuttgart company had recently designed and developed a two-litre, water-cooled, FR (front engine, rear-wheel drive) sports car for Volkswagen, the commission coming officially in January 1972 when the VG was still active. Almost from

the moment the 914 was launched, Volkswagen had been considering the details for its more conventional successor, and the EA-425 (or Type 924 as it became in Porsche terminology) was to be it, although badged as an Audi to fit in with the then-current VW-Audi-Porsche marketing arrangements.

Testing began, and by spring 1974 tooling was being purchased in readiness for building the new model. However, at the last minute, just as the machine had reached the pre-production stage, the management at Volkswagen cancelled it due to a combination of political wrangling and the energy crisis. The consensus at VW was that it would be too expensive to produce, and the Karmann-built Scirocco was sufficient to cater for the small sports car sector of the market (it was developed alongside the Golf under contract number EA-337).

Porsche was given the opportunity to buy back the EA-425 design to put it into production itself, which it did gladly, even though it cost a reputed DM160 million. The deal was concluded in January 1975, by which time Volkswagen had already spent DM180 million in development and initial tooling costs.

The 924 was exactly what Porsche

needed in the hard economic times of the 1970s. As mentioned in Chapter Two, the 914 was offered in two-litre form only for the 1976 model year (powered by a modified VW unit), and even then, only in the States – it was the only affordable route to Porsche ownership. Sales had fallen off considerably, and just 9424 cars were produced in Stuttgart in 1975.

The 911 continued to be updated satisfactorily, and, as a result, although the 928 project had been started earlier, it would be the 924 that reached the market first. At last Porsche had the entry level machine it had originally been trying to acquire with the 914.

A new Porsche

Jochen Freund was the Project Director, reporting directly to Paul Hensler, who had overall responsibility for the development of the 924. Having joined Porsche in 1958, he became chief of the Experimental Department after Helmuth Bott was promoted. They had a great deal of work ahead of them before the new car could be launched.

As Volkswagen had commissioned the new sporting coupé for the Audi line, naturally enough a high proportion of

the components had been sourced from Wolfsburg. Historically speaking, this was nothing new for the Stuttgart firm, but, in its mechanical layout, the 924 represented a great departure from traditional Porsche practice.

Most of the Volkswagen range had moved to front-wheel drive, but for a traditional sporting vehicle the FF layout was simply not acceptable – at least, not at that time. Although it was perfect in poor weather conditions, it didn't offer the same level of driver control one expects from a Porsche. Besides, if the company wanted to develop more powerful versions in the future, there was always going to be a limit imposed by the tyres having to steer the car and put down power at the same time. A heavier, water-cooled engine mounted at the rear was also far from ideal, and the MR layout (as in the 914) had proved unsatisfactory.

The mid-engine layout, despite a reputation for twitchy handling at the limits, wasn't the problem per se; indeed, the 911 had a similar reputation, but Porsche happily persevered with the design. In any case, most people knew their own limits, which, thankfully, were much lower than those of the vehicle. No, the biggest problem, apart from servicing difficulties, was a distinct lack of interior accommodation and luggage space. The 914's replacement had to be more practical.

A traditional FR layout seemed the only logical way to go, employing a transaxle system (a combined gearbox and rear axle unit) to aid weight distribution and traction.

Dr Fuhrmann and his team of engineers had specified the transaxle arrangement for the new 928, so it seemed sensible to adopt it on the smaller model as well.

Porsche was offered the new five-cylinder, 2144cc Audi 100 powerplant with a view to possibly making a V10 from it for the 928. Instead, Porsche decided to use the latest four-cylinder Audi 100 engine (due for introduction in the 1977 MY, which also found its way into the all-new VW LT commercial vehicle and the AMC Gremlin) as the starting point because, at two-litres (a bore and stroke of 86.5 x 84.4mm resulted in a displacement of 1984cc), it gave a perfect cubic capacity for a small sports car from a taxation point of view. Some markets, such as Italy and Japan, impose a very heavy tax on cars with an engine of over two-litres, and this was supposed to be an entry-level model, after all.

Another less obvious reason was

that Porsche didn't want to rely too heavily on VW supplies – with their relationship going soar, it wasn't a good idea to have the 928 engine (remember, the 928 was the proposed replacement for the 911) and a large number of parts for what would be the only other car in the range for the foreseeable future, the 924, being sourced from the VW-Audi empire.

Some would have you believe that the 924 power unit was lifted straight from the VW LT van, when, in fact, there were a number of important differences. With its belt-driven ohc running in a crossflow aluminium alloy head, the standard Audi-developed, four-cylinder engine employed carburettors, whilst the Porsche powerplant (designated XK) was equipped with Bosch K-Jetronic fuel-injection, making it more suitable for anti-pollution devices.

The cast-iron block was retained, playing host to a forged five-bearing

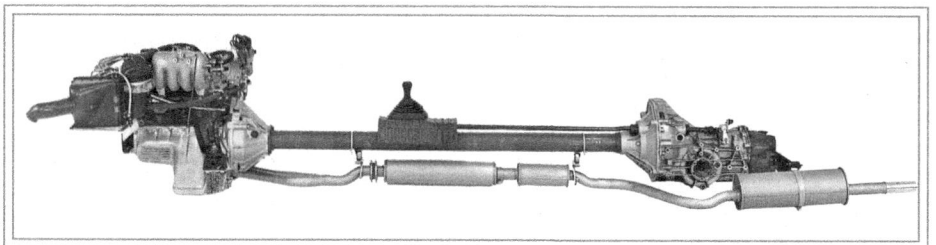

The Porsche transaxle arrangement. The original works caption read: "The transaxle unit of the Porsche 924 forms – by means of a sturdy 'backbone' tube – a rigid unit. The principle of the transaxle, with the engine in front and transmission and differential in the rear, ensures well-balanced weight distribution and neutral driving characteristics under any load conditions." Note the three silencers on the European specification exhaust system.

crankshaft, but the cylinder head featured rotating eccentric, wedge-type adjusters on the cam-followers instead of shims (European specification engines had 40mm inlet valves, and 33mm diameter exhaust valves). A compression ratio of 9.3:1 (the same as that for the Audi 100 application) meant a definite need for four-star fuel (98 octane rating), but with these refinements, it resulted in a reliable 125bhp – an improvement of 10bhp over the Audi four, and just 11bhp short of the heavier five-cylinder unit in high-output form.

This maximum power figure, developed at 5800rpm, was fairly modest, as was the torque output – 121.5lbft at 3500rpm – but in the fuel crisis era, performance had to be seen to be balanced with economy. Even Jaguar introduced a 3.4 litre engine to augment its 4.2 and 5.3 litre units in the face of rising energy concerns. Besides, these figures compared favourably with the original Porsche two-litre sixes and the outgoing ohv four found in the 914, and torque was plentiful from fairly low down the rev range.

To allow a lower bonnet line the engine was canted over 40 degrees to the right, and moved as far back as possible in the bay to help improve weight distribution, and thus enhance the car's handling; this necessitated a new aluminium alloy sump, which was duly given cooling fins to help keep oil temperature down.

The K-Jetronic fuel-injection system was chosen over the newer L-Jetronic set-up, incidentally, because the former was largely mechanical, and could therefore be repaired more readily by a non-specialist workshop; this incorporated an electric fuel pump.

Cooling was provided by water, of course, the pump being driven by a V-belt which also operated the 75 amp alternator's pulley (there was a cover on the alternator, incidentally, to direct cooling air and keep it free of dirt). The radiator was a sealed unit, employing a small separate header tank (made of clear plastic, it was situated centrally in front of the engine), while a thermostatically-controlled electric fan reduced noise and a needless drain of horsepower – if the engine was hot, the fan continued to run after the ignition was switched off, a further advantage of an electric fan. In the interests of keeping as much weight as possible within the wheelbase up front, the battery was mounted in the scuttle area.

As mentioned earlier, to take power to the rear wheels, Porsche opted for a transaxle arrangement. It wasn't a new idea (Grand Prix cars used the system extensively during the 1930s and '50s) but, despite its undoubted advantages, it was rare on a road car. Alfa Romeo had just introduced the Alfetta range, which incorporated a transaxle, but after a great deal of research Porsche took a slightly different approach to its Milanese competitor.

The engineers in Stuttgart were not overly happy with the quality of the gearchange in other transaxle-equipped vehicles. Using the Alfa as a perfect example, the gear linkage was long, and propshaft inertia – due to the rear-mounted clutch – put a lot of stress on the synchromesh.

To overcome the problem, Porsche kept the clutch attached to the engine flywheel, with power being taken to the rear-mounted transmission via a high quality, slim (and therefore low-mass) 20mm steel bar. This small diameter bar would normally be too whippy, so the clever part was to run it within an 85mm diameter tube with four strategically placed, sealed-for-life ball bearings, and then use this tube to connect one Audi fwd bell-housing at the front, bolted to the engine, and another at the rear, attached to the gearbox. This tube effectively kept the engine and gearbox as a single unit, maintaining a perfectly straight driveline, and provided a solid mounting for the gearchange and linkage (which found its way to the transmission through an aperture in the rear bell-housing), as well as a handy support for the exhaust system.

To test the theory of Porsche's transaxle arrangement in the early stages of development, a BMW 2002 was fitted with the Audi engine and modified drivetrain (the suspension was also evaluated in this car); later, Opel Mantas, with their similar wheelbase, would serve as mules. Anyway, having owned both an Alfa GTV and a 924, the author can confirm that Porsche's approach was undoubtedly the better one in this case, at least for the majority of drivers. Shifts were substantially

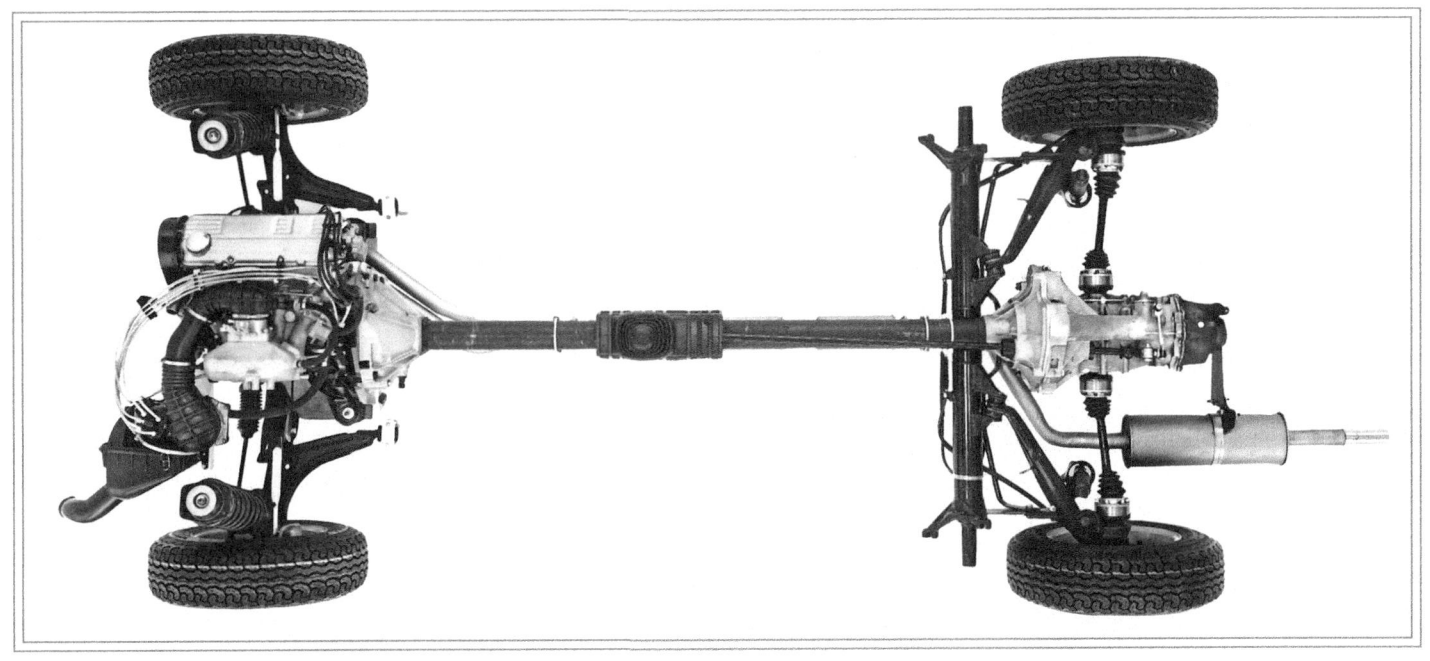

Overhead view of the 924 layout, showing engine, transmission and suspension.

quicker, due, perhaps, as much to the shorter gearlever, and definitely more precise by a massive margin, although I must say that gearchanges felt more involving with the Italian car. It comes down to personal taste, of course, but for me, the 924 'box was just too easy to use – too remote. But then ease of use is what most manufacturers strive for, and should never be classed as a disadvantage, except by those with a warped sense of humour.

Ultimately, in addition to better gearchange quality, the transaxle arrangement, with just two mountings required at either end, afforded a very rigid structure, good balance (weight distribution was 48% front, 52% rear), excellent traction (thanks to the subtle rearward bias) and enhanced crash protection at both ends – a front impact could be partially absorbed by the tube, while a rear-end shunt could push the bell-housing only a limited amount before it fouled with the body. It was, quite literally, a stroke of genius.

The gearbox itself was sourced from Audi. Designated the Type O-88 transmission, it was an all-synchromesh, four-speed manual unit (the ratios being 3.60:1 on first,

2.12:1 on second, 1.36:1 on third and a slightly overdriven 0.97:1 top), with a 3.44:1 hypoid bevel final drive; a cable-operated, single dry plate clutch was employed.

Front suspension was by MacPherson struts and coil springs (as used on the VW Golf), with stronger lower A-arms coming from the Scirocco, whilst the rear suspension incorporated semi-trailing arms with transverse torsion bars. It was basically the same as the 911's, except that it employed parts sourced from the Volkswagen Super Beetle! The rack-and-pinion steering was also from VW, being based on the Scirocco unit, with a collapsible column and four turns lock-to-lock. Interestingly, despite the car's sporting nature, to keep the price down, both front and rear anti-roll bars (20 and 18mm diameter respectively) were listed as an option.

Driveshafts came from the VW Type 181 cross-country vehicle, and braking was via 257mm diameter solid discs with Audi floating calipers at the front and 230mm diameter drums at the rear, the latter providing the best set-up for a good handbrake (these were sourced from the VW K70

Anatole 'Tony' Lapine – Porsche's amiable Chief Designer. Although much of the 924's design has been credited to Harm Lagaay, ultimately, final responsibility for the project rested with Lapine.

model); servo-assistance was standard, with the hydraulic circuits being split diagonally. The handbrake lever, incidentally, was placed between the driver's seat and the sill – some people complained in later test reports, but in my years of 924 ownership (as well as those with the Jaguar XJ-S, which

Eight prototypes were built for testing during 1973 and '74.

The original lines were much heavier than the production model, displaying a distinct likeness in many respects to the forthcoming 928.

had a similar arrangement), I must say that it never bothered me.

Clothing this mechanical cocktail was an elegant body designed by 29 year old Dutchman, Harm Lagaay, although the ultimate responsibility lay with Tony Lapine, Porsche's Chief Designer, who oversaw the project. Lapine was born in Latvia in 1930, and spent 17 years with General Motors, working alongside top stylist Bill Mitchell in the States before being assigned to Opel (part of the GM empire). Whilst in Germany, Porsche offered him a position; after Butzi

Early prototypes had a heavy frame around the rear window, but this was later discarded. Porsche had thought of using a large glass hatch before, but this was the first time it had been seen on a production car from the Stuttgart concern. It could only be opened by a key (the same one used for the ignition), but was supported by two gas struts, which would actually help lift the glass panel – a heater element was standard for all markets. A certain amount of care had to be taken when closing the hatch, however, as the two locating pins had to be pushed home evenly. Note the rear lights.

An early prototype in profile. The rear flanks were very heavy-looking at this stage, the design completely lacking the elegance of the production car.

Two of the first eight prototypes. The vehicle on the right had been used for a forward-impact crash test. Although it looks far from happy, in reality, it has survived well, as the passenger cell is still pretty much untouched.

helped aerodynamics but was also aesthetically pleasing." The Cd was just 0.36, a very good figure for the mid-1970s, and one which would help promote good fuel economy.

In an interview conducted in 1979, Lapine stated that although the design had been produced for Volkswagen, the "924 is a Porsche through and through. We'd never give the customer last year's know-how. We always give our best because that drives you to greatness." He added that the only things changed during the VW-Audi to Porsche transformation process were the badges on the nose and steering wheel boss, and the ignition key.

Compared with many of its contemporaries, the 924 had a timeless look about it. In America, by far the biggest market for this kind of car, the pure lines of the Datsun Z were being spoilt by the onslaught of Federal regulations, while others like Alfa Romeo and Lotus adopted the straight-edge styling that was very much en vogue at the time. The Mazda RX-7 had yet to appear, of course (it made its Japanese debut in March 1978), while of the US makers, vehicles in this category just seemed to lack the elegance and subtlety of the Porsche. Naturally, some of the Italian exotics were more stunning, but so were their prices ...

The front wings could be unbolted for quick and easy replacement, and the rear body panels, sills and floorpan were galvanized to protect the vehicle from corrosion; a new welding material was developed to stop rusting at the joints, a vulnerable area. As a result, the 924 was given the same six-year,

Porsche left the family fold, Lapine assumed the mantle of head of styling and design.

The new Porsche was a wedge-shaped 2+2 coupé with smooth lines and a large glass hatch at the rear. Even today it looks surprisingly modern, thanks to some fine detailing; pop-up headlights kept the airflow clean over the front-end, while cooling air to the radiator was directed through

the smallest of slots underneath the number plate.

"We asked our engineers for two things." said Lapine. "Firstly, we wanted to have the hood so low that the view ahead would be as unimpeded as it is in a rear-engined car. And secondly, we didn't want any large apertures in the front. As a result, even those for the water-cooling were kept exceedingly small, which not only

After the body shape was finalized via a full-sized clay model, wind tunnel testing was done via a fibreglass mock-up taken off the clay. This put the finishing touches to the design.

anti-perforation guarantee as the 911.

The pop-up headlights were raised as soon as the sidelights were switched on, operated by a single motor (actually a wiper motor!) to save weight and money, coupled by a simple linkage which worked via a cam. Turning off the ignition automatically cut the headlights, leaving only the sidelights on so as not to drain the battery.

Fairly boring pressed steel 5.5-inch wheels were supplied as standard, fitted with 165 x 14 tyres; the optional 6J, eight-spoke, cast-aluminium alloys, which came with low-profile 185/70 x 14 HR-rated tyres, lifted the appearance of the vehicle no end, making the car look much better. Both had a four-stud fitting, the alloys weighing just 13.5lbs each (6.1kg).

Inside, the comfortable high-back seats were sourced from the 911, with a fine range of fore and aft adjustment, and a release lever on the side giving access to the two rear seats without upsetting the desired angle of the backrest. The rear seats, unique to

Another six prototypes were built corresponding to the final design. The original caption on the back of this photograph calls the new model "A Swabian Prince of Darkness."

the 924, were really for children, or occasional use by adults (leg- and headroom was somewhat restricted). In all fairness, the car was described as a 2+2 rather than a full four-seater. A practical feature was the ability to fold the rear seat to increase luggage capacity and allow longer loads to be carried.

In front of the driver there were three main large circular gauges: a central speedometer (calibrated to either 150mph or 250kph depending on market), a tachometer on the right

(marked up to 8000rpm, despite the red band starting at 6500rpm), and a combined temperature and fuel gauge of the same diameter on the left; it also contained warning lights for the battery, handbrake, low fuel and oil pressure, and excessive coolant temperature. Interestingly, instruments were fitted with conical lenses in an attempt to eliminate reflection.

Two stalks on the steering column provided controls for the indicators/ flash/dip and windscreen washer/ wipers, while rocker switches for the lights, heated rear window and hazard warning lights were mounted beyond them on the main instrument panel. The centre console was added at the last minute, housing a clock and matching gauges for oil pressure and oil temperature. Separate tell-tales were supplied for brake fluid loss and

Rear three-quarter view of one of the six final prototypes. The rear flanks have been completely revised and are now much neater, while the combination lamps have been made into a styling feature.

The whole design was much lighter, and some felt it was too dainty. Fortunately, the general concensus was that Lapine and his men had done a good job. It will be noted that there were no badges anywhere on this prototype vehicle.

excessive pad wear, placed alongside a standard cigarette lighter. A stereo could be fitted in the lower section, just below the heating controls.

The heating and ventilation system came from the Golf with water valve control (face-level vents were provided in the centre and at both ends of the moulded fascia), although stale air was extracted in a novel way: ducts underneath the rear hatch drew air into channels which routed it into the doors. The air was then extracted through a concealed vent at the leading edge of each door, a natural

49

Cold weather testing with a 924 on Heilbronn trade plates, as opposed to the 'S' number allocated to Stuttgart.

always be folded to give ample space if owners weren't too worried about their cargo being seen. Either way, it was hardly a massive advantage over the 914, although the occasional rear seats were undoubtedly handy.

Engines were to be built at VW's Salzgitter works, and transmissions produced at Kassel; the body was

low-pressure area when the car is moving at speed. This, it was claimed, not only kept the rear window clear of condensation, but also kept the doors warm in colder weather.

Door panels were fully-trimmed, with little bins under the combination armrest/door pulls, although much of the door furniture was the same as that used for the VW Scirocco. Aft of the gearlever was a covered ashtray, with switches for the driving lights and, when fitted, the foglights and rear wiper.

As for luggage space, well, there wasn't that much, although the author and his wife managed a trek across Europe without too much trouble. The biggest problem was the height of the transaxle, which left a very shallow boot if the retractable cover (fitted from August 1976) was to be used, and the spare wheel, placed upright at the rear of the car, also encroached on what little room there was.

However, small compartments on either side of the luggage area (between the rear wheelarches and rear light housings) provided useful hiding places for valuables, and the rear seat could

An early interior for the home market. Many journalists complained that the interior was too basic. Fortunately, initial plans to market an even simpler model were rejected, otherwise the press would have had a field day. Despite lock-to-lock requiring four turns, the 924 had a turning circle of considerably less than ten metres; very impressive for a car of this type, and a facet which is appreciated more with time. Note the way the fascia blended into the door cappings – quite a modern feature.

Engines were built and tested at Volkswagen's Salzgitter factory.

Bodyshell production at the former NSU factory in Neckarsulm, where final assembly also took place. Porsche executives were always full of praise for the NSU workers, who were very experienced in building specialist vehicles following several years spent producing the Ro80.

Transmissions were built up at Kassel in another VW-Audi plant. Synchromesh surfaces had a molybdenum coating to improve performance and longevity.

51

NSU workers preparing a 924 bodyshell for painting. Quality control was monitored by Porsche's own staff.

constructed at the former NSU factory at Neckarsulm, where main assembly took place, albeit under Porsche supervision (it was only a few minutes north of Stuttgart). Interestingly, Mercedes-Benz was also negotiating with Volkswagen at that time to have the W123-series estates built at Neckarsulm. Considering that the future of the plant had hung in the balance only months before, this new-found flood of work was most welcome.

After about 100 pilot-build cars had been built, full production started in November. It was originally scheduled at 80 cars a day, with a maximum capacity of around 100 units – fractionally less than that of the 914 in its heyday.

The 1976 MY for America

The two-litre 914 was offered initially, but was soon replaced by the 912E – the 912 being the very model that the 914 was introduced to replace! However, while the Porsche 912 had the four-cylinder, 1.6-litre, Type 616/36 or 616/39 engine (the latter being for California), the 912E was powered by the fuel-injected, two-litre, Type 923/02 unit, and was only ever sold in the US.

Though this situation was somewhat ironic, it meant dealers

Paul Hensler – the man in charge of the 924 project.

As a stop-gap between the 914 and 924, Porsche introduced the 912E for the American market's 1976 model year.

had a lower-priced machine with which to bridge the gap following the demise of the 914, and the wait for the forthcoming 924. As *Road & Track* noted: "the 912E will obviously find favour with those who prefer a slightly more practical and tractable Porsche. It's a car with almost all the sporting virtues of the more expensive 911S, yet its simpler pushrod four-cylinder engine should make for better fuel economy and less expensive maintenance than the 911's six."

The 923/02 engine was basically the same as that found in the later two-litre 914, but with the L-Jetronic fuel-injection system found on the earlier 1.8-litre models. With just 86bhp on tap, performance was more than respectable – *Road & Track* recorded a top speed of 115mph and a 0-60 time of 11.5 seconds.

Various mechanical aspects of the vehicle were simplified to keep production costs down (such as fitting a front anti-roll bar only, and using solid rather than ventilated disc brakes), as well as a number of features in interior specification. Otherwise – especially if the optional Fuchs alloy wheels were fitted – it was hard to tell a 912E from a 911S.

Although short-lived, according to the chassis numbers (which ran from 9126000001 to 9126002099), a total of 2099 912Es were built, all during the 1976 model year, and all destined for American shores. There it sold for $10,845, exactly $3000 cheaper than a 911S coupé, but some $3600 more expensive than the two-litre 914. In the meantime, a totally new Porsche had

been launched in Germany.

Launch of the 924

The Frankfurt Show is traditionally held in September. The theme of the 1973 event was 'Into the future with the automobile', but the oil crisis sparked off by the Arab-Israeli conflict left a big question mark over the future of the car. As such, the theme of the next Frankfurt Show (which ran from 11 to 21 September 1975) was 'Live better with the automobile'.

There was very little in the way of exotic machinery at the German event, reflecting the overriding atmosphere of the period. However, the Porsche 911 Turbo made its first appearance at Frankfurt, Jaguar launched the XJ-S and Mercedes displayed the 450SEL 6.9, so it wasn't all economy cars or warmed-up versions of existing models.

For some, the two-litre machine would have been something of an anti-climax. Rumours of a five-litre V8 Grand Tourer had been circulating around the industry for quite a while. Spy shots had shown this much talked about project to be similar to the 924 in profile, but where was that long-awaited engine everyone was expecting? Even the more informed members of the Press had a twin-cam conversion of the Audi 100 unit in mind, so the appearance of an sohc four, much the same as the Audi's on the face of it, meant the air of disappointment would have been too much to bear on home soil. Partly for this reason, and partly to get the undivided attention of the Press, the car was launched a couple of months later in opulent

surroundings in the South of France.

According to tests carried out at Weissach, the 924 could achieve the same lateral acceleration figures as a standard 911 (0.872g), and was significantly quicker than a 914 over the Mountain Test Course. Factory performance figures listed a 125mph top speed, with 0-60 coming up in 10.5 seconds – fractionally slower than a 914/6 but an improvement on the outgoing two-litre 914. Average fuel consumption was said to work out at an amazing 36mpg – with a light right foot, I'd be inclined to agree with this, and Porsche's performance quotes have always had a reputation for being conservative.

As for dimensions, the length was 4200mm (with a wheelbase of 2400mm), and height and width were 1270 and 1685mm respectively. The track was quoted at 1418mm at the front and 1372mm at the rear, and ground clearance was 150mm; kerb weight was listed as being 2376lbs (1080kg). The fuel tank, incidentally, had a capacity of 13.6 Imperial gallons, or 62 litres.

Major options – other than those covered earlier in the chapter – included a rear window wiper, high-pressure headlight washers, and a removable fibreglass roof panel which could be stored in the boot. Naturally, a range of stereo equipment could be selected, with provision for speakers in the centre of the upper part of the fascia and in the panels to the sides of the rear seats.

It was also stated that an automatic transmission would be offered in the near future, which

A beautiful publicity shot taken near La Grand Motte.

At the time of its launch, an array of optional equipment was promised for the 924: a removable roof panel, seen here in prototype form (strangely, cars with this option were actually more rigid than closed models as there was a strengthening ring in the roof) ...

... high-pressure headlamp
washers ...

*... and a rear wiper and roof rack
being on the list; an automatic
gearbox was also on the cards. Note
the 'Porsche' decals running along the
sill line, an option offered from day
one in all markets.*

delighted a number of potential owners (especially in America), but left just as many Porsche purists wondering what had become of their highly-prized marque.

Early press reaction

The press launch was held at the La Grande Motte resort in the picturesque Camargue area of France in November 1975. During the customary speech, it was stated: "We are not bound to any concept, we are just bound to make any concept work better than others." But what did the press think?

The *Autocar* stated: "Though the configuration of the 924 may make it sound like a 'bitsa' car, the whole effect is harmonious, and obviously well-engineered."

Initially, *Road & Track* described the styling as "conservative," adding that "available photos of the car do not bespeak an exciting shape but rather a practical, somewhat predated one." It would be fair to say that the magazine was not overly impressed but, fortunately for Porsche, its views regarding this aspect of the design were not shared by the majority; some went as far as to call the 924 "a beautiful shape" once they had seen the real

thing. Proof of the design's acceptance, if proof were needed, came in the form of several styling accolades.

Of the power unit, Jerry Sloniger wrote: "The Audi engine sings up to its red-line with a proper sporting note but is more noteable for elasticity so that they could easily gear it nice and long for effortless cruising." An article in *Motor Sport* echoed this view, describing the unit as "smooth, willing and flexible." However, not all reports on the engine were complementary

(rather an understatement), but more of that later.

As for the gearbox, surprisingly, the synchromesh on the early cars wasn't Porsche's fabled design, but most people appreciated the depth of engineering behind the 924's transaxle. "Here again is an example of the usual Porsche attention to mechanical detail," said Road Test. "The shifter ... works flawlessly, with short, precise throws and no slop in the linkage. The shift linkage in the 911 doesn't have

An interesting shot which clearly shows the very clean aerodynamic lines of the 924. A series of photographs were taken of this car for the press hand-outs.

to reach nearly as far and it is only a fraction as good."

Autocar was equally impressed, noting: "The result is a quite delightful, short-action, positive gearchange." It added: "There is no lost movement or vagueness, no torque reaction fed through the gearlever, and no delay while a heavy propshaft is brought to rest by the synchromesh."

Having had the chance to try an early car fitted with the optional alloy wheels, wider 185/70 tyres and anti-roll bars, the venerable John Bolster observed: "The cornering power is very high, the car getting round without a sign of roll or tyre scream. It's a bit hard to judge cornering speeds at first, for the 924 gives no indication that one is approaching the limit. However, few owners are likely to get anywhere near this point, the great reserve of cornering power being a real safety feature. Bumps do not throw the car off its line and the traction is exceptional,

with a remarkable absence of wheelspin during acceleration on first gear."

Although "moderate roll" was noted during cornering, "the chassis behaviour would do credit to Colin Chapman," said *Motor Sport*. Indeed, most described the handling as perfectly neutral, with slight understeer on the limit, but the ride certainly came in for a lot of criticism. However, few found fault with the steering, *Road & Track* noting: "The steering is light and quick and you put the car where you want it."

The brakes were also almost universally praised. John Bolster of *Autosport* reported: "The brakes are very potent and can achieve some remarkable crash-stops without skidding the wheels; they give a splendid feeling of security, compared with too many modern brakes, which lack 'bite' in sudden emergencies. The handbrake is well up to its work, too."

Overall, performance was adequate

("it accelerates acceptably, but if there was any less [power] it would be noticeably slow," said Road Test), whilst economy was generally vastly superior to that of its contemporary competitors.

An interesting comment was made in *Autocar*: "In a way it would be easy to call the 924 characterless. The adrenalin does not flow, yet that is its strength, able to travel quietly, quickly, and very safely over long distances."

Sadly, it wasn't all good news. Some people noted the quite wide gap between the lower gears, but it should be borne in mind that, to make a special five-speed gearbox just for the 924, would have wiped out much of the model's price advantage over its 911 stablemate. However, this was a minor problem compared to some others expressed by journalists from around the world.

Ride and NVH control seemed to be the major bones of contention in an otherwise thoroughly acceptable

Atmospheric shot of the 924 just beyond the tail of the three-litre 911 Carrera.

The new car pictured at Mont St Michel in Brittany. The sidelights and indicators were recessed in the fibreglass front bumper, giving the car a very clean look. On European models, the facility to 'flash' oncoming vehicles was transferred to the driving lights when the headlights were down. Note the small rubber over-riders on each side of the front number plate.

package. *Motor Sport* described the ride as "harsh," adding "there is far too much wind and mechanical noise, accompanied by a great deal of tyre and suspension roar and thump."

Several people noted that the interior was rather stark given the price of the car, and that the rear seats were something of a joke if the people up front were to be comfortable. A far greater worry was that the slightly oval steering wheel was placed much too low for most, with no adjustment to move it up out of the way.

Poor fresh air ventilation was also cited in a number of publications. In addition, after 12,000 miles with the 924, Jeremy Sinek commented in *Motor* that the heating system had "a mind of its own. Ultimately very powerful, the heater output is far more responsive to the speed that the car is travelling at than to adjustments of the temperature control slider."

Writing for *Road & Track*, Ron Wakefield mentioned: "The driving position is not one of its strengths ... I found it too low: the sloping hood drops completely out of sight for me and lacks defined corners anyway, so even when I leaned forward parking was chancy. Driving vision, conversely, is good except that those shorter

drivers may also have trouble with the high lower ledges of the wrapped-over rear window. The pedals are way forward, the steering wheel low and not adjustable; I bumped my knees against it when clutching and braking, something that usually happens to tall people."

Only *Road Test* seemed to think otherwise, stating that "the seating and driving position were superb ... the steering wheel position is right on

and they have thoughtfully arranged the pedals so that when the brake is down it is on the same level as the throttle, making heel-and-toeing a snap." On the subject of pedals, Porsche provided a footrest to the left of the clutch, a thoughtful touch much appreciated when cruising a motorway or autobahn.

The engine was another problem. "Mechanical refinement is lacking at the top end of the engine's range,"

Interior of the 1976 model year 924 for the home market. At this stage, door panels were trimmed in vinyl to match the leatherette used on the seats. The window winder was a necessity, as electric windows had yet to be offered; when they were, in late 1977, the switches were located on the door cappings, close to the fascia. The rear quarter windows were fixed, incidentally.

The 924 was not only pretty, but practical, too. Although this is obviously a staged shot for publicity purposes, the author and his wife used to go shopping regularly without any real problems.

reported *Autocar*. "There's no missing the engine's Audi heritage," said Ron Wakefield in another publication. "It's a bit on the rough and noisy side."

A lack of power was another gripe shared by many (including me, it has to be said), but, compared to its true rivals in the two-litre class, the 924 could happily hold its own. For instance, a Ford Capri GT had only 99bhp, the Lancia Beta Montecarlo

only 120bhp and the Triumph TR7 a measly 92. Only the Alfa GTV and the Lotus Esprit (at 131 and 156bhp, respectively) could produce more power with the same displacement,

Maybe the 924 didn't have the same glamour as the 911, but the series would go on to provide more than 140,000 people with good, enjoyable service by the time it was discontinued. Cheaper running costs made it the sensible Porsche for the younger owner or family man.

but on paper they were no quicker off the mark and paid for this additional power with increased fuel consumption.

Undoubtedly, the 924 was not without its faults, but the biggest problem in my opinion was people's perceived image of Porsche – surely a car wearing the fabled Porsche badge should be able to perform better?

The introduction of the 924 certainly caused one or two ripples (to say the least!), as Porsche fanatics could proudly boast of the race victories taken by the 917 and the fantastic turn of speed that the 911 Turbo had. But, in reality, how many of those people actually owned a 911 Turbo, or even driven one, for that matter?

An enviable reputation is a wonderful thing, but Porsche, like all manufacturers, has to sell cars to survive. It's all very well a journalist saying that a 911 is better in this way and far superior in that – in the real world few can afford one; if they could, 10 per cent of the entire population would have one, and by now it would have become one of the best-selling vehicle's of all time.

There is simply no point in trying to compare a 924 with a 911 Turbo – the 924 was introduced to cater for an entirely different type of buyer, and to bring Porsche motoring to a wider audience at reasonable cost. From the outset, their objectives were completely different.

Besides, broadening a range has never adversely affected the likes of Mercedes or BMW. For years, Benz happily sold diesel vans alongside

such beauties as the 450SLC, whilst BMW listed a 1.6 litre 3-series – a total contrast to the sporting 3.5 litre, fuel-injected, 6-series coupé. And everyone seems to have conveniently forgotten that the creator of the 'Ultimate Driving Machine' once made bubble cars!

Ultimately, the 924 was brought into the Porsche range because of financial reality: without a cheaper entry level model, the marque simply couldn't survive. The 914 had received the same frosty reception, but, at the end of the day, it went on to be Porsche's best-selling model by quite some margin. Would the 924 be able to overcome this initial animosity? Only time would tell, but in traditional Porsche fashion, problems – the real problems–would be tackled one by one.

The 924 became available on the home market first, early examples filtering into the showrooms during February 1976, with prices starting at DM23,240. Production at this time was limited to around 60 units per day, but as orders from the US and UK markets flooded in, this figure was soon increased.

The contemporary 911s
The six-cylinder engine of the 911 range was constantly upgraded; from 2.2 litres for 1970, to 2.4 litres or 1972, and 2.7 litres for 1974; the Carrera ultimately came a three-litre unit. The 911 Turbo appeared at the 1974 Paris Salon, taking the world by storm with its electrifying performance. Not only was this the quickest road car to come from the Stuttgart factory during that period, it was also the most expensive,

Contemporary 911s. From left to right: the 911 coupé, the Carrera in Targa form and the legendary 911 Turbo. In reality, like the 914 before it, the 924 would have to wait a very long time before traditional Porsche enthusiasts (i.e. 911 buyers) would give it a greeting like this.

One of a series of publicity shots taken for a preliminary six-page American catalogue. When the car first appeared in the States, Motor Trend noted: "There is no doubt the Porsche 924 is just about what its makers intended it to be: not a refined GT machine, but a modern sports car."

at nearly twice the price of a 911S coupé. However, despite a hefty price tag and the relentless rise in fuel costs, within 18 months of its launch, Porsche had already sold twice the number originally expected.

For the 1976 model year, the European specification 2687cc units were given more power until the normally-aspirated range was standardized at three-litres for 1978. At the same time, the Turbo became a 3.3 litre unit developing a hefty 300bhp. Meanwhile, the range had been simplified to allow for the addition of another new car to join the Porsche line-up – the 928.

The 924 hits America

The 924 was scheduled for a July 1976 launch in the US, but arrived three months earlier (at this stage, with advance orders flooding in from all corners of the globe, production reached a peak of 109 cars per day at one point). Classed as a 1977 model year vehicle, it replaced the 912E in the line-up; at just $9395 it was some $4600 cheaper than a 911S coupé, and over $1000 cheaper than the short-lived model it superseded.

As for options, the $345 Touring Package I comprised alloy wheels with wider 185/70 tyres (these alone were $295 if bought separately), three speakers, an aerial, suppression kit and leather steering wheel cover. Touring Package II, priced at $240, included headlight washers, a second outside mirror and a rear wiper; other options included air conditioning ($548), metallic paint ($295), the sunroof ($330), anti-roll bars ($105) and various stereo systems.

To comply with Federal emissions regulations, air injection and EGR (exhaust gas recirculation) systems were employed in the XH 49-State versions, with catalytic converters taking the place of an air pump for California cars (the latter, designated XF and also supplied to Japan, naturally dictating the use of unleaded fuel); the compression ratio was reduced to just 8.0:1 via different shaped piston crowns, and smaller diameter inlet valves were used. This saw a drop in power to just 95bhp at 5500rpm, and a corresponding reduction in maximum torque output, quoted at 109lbft at 3000rpm for American specification models.

Apart from a distinct lack of horses under the bonnet, with breakerless transistorised ignition, at least the engine was easy to start and had excellent driveability, which was more than could be said for a lot of rival powerplants from the mid-1970s in detoxed guise.

"There is nothing fussy about the engine," said *Motor Trend*, "and you can get into fourth gear on a 35mph street, although third gives better response in that situation. For that matter, even second will get you over the national speed limit if you don't mind twisting it a bit. The engine will easily exceed the 6500rpm red line, but it tends to let you know that things are getting tight at anything more than 5500rpm by emitting a harmonic-like buzz. There's no high rpm song here, just in-line four-cylinder noises."

Road & Track noted that "the

Right: Another view of the US specification car with its different bumper arrangement. From this angle, it's obvious that the final design was much less bulbous than the original, but it was still far from slab-sided.

shifter is very good for a transaxle car," but the gearing was the same as that for the European market. Consequently, with tall gears, additional weight (the larger bumpers and emissions equipment brought the vehicle up to 2410lbs/1095kg in the States) and less power on tap, *Motor Trend* recorded a rather disappointing 0-60mph time of 12.6 seconds, breaking through the quarter-mile marker 5.9 seconds later at a terminal speed of just under 74mph. However, the car pulled a very impressive 0.82g on the skidpan (it was fitted with the optional front and rear anti-roll bars, incidentally), and also established some noteworthy fuel consumption figures.

From the earliest days side rubbing strips were a feature on some US cars, fitted (with varying levels of competence, it has to be said) in the States. From August 1976 production, all cars came with these as standard, along with a voltmeter in place of the original oil temperature gauge. The obligatory US side markers are ugly in the author's opinion, especially on this side of the car where, combined with the exposed fuel cap, the design looks too cluttered. The markers ruined the 924's clean, simple lines.

Road Test managed to get the 0-60 time down to 11.6 seconds and shaved a fraction off the standing-quarter yardstick, but with over 25lbs (11.5kg) to move for every one of the 95 horsepower compared with only 19lbs (8.6kg) for the European specification model, it was obvious where the performance disparity came from. Maximum speeds through the gears, incidentally, were 36, 60, 93 and 111mph.

In the August 1976 issue, *Motor Trend* noted: "The car doesn't feel fast ... Travelling with traffic that is moving at the national highway average of around 62mph, the 924 feels like it's doing about 50, even though it is picking up on the other cars on the road. It's deceptive, but is also the mark of a good sports car, an attribute found in most of the world's truly fast touring cars – especially Porsches."

The following month Road Test looked at the new Porsche. Regarding

handling it said: "The car works far better than a 911. It has slightly lower limits but it is vastly more predictable at those limits. At the skidpan the standard car would go around at 0.78g and was near-neutral with the throttle on. Backing off the gas caused the back end to come around, but the car went to the inside of the circle instead of, like the 911 will do, to the outside. We also tried a 924 with the optional suspension pieces (20mm front anti-roll bar, 18mm rear bar, six-inch wide alloy wheels and 185/70 HR14 tyres) and it went around consistently at 0.81g with occasional laps above that. It was, compared to the 911 and especially the Turbo, much more controllable at the limit and nearly as fast.

"What we couldn't evaluate about the chassis was the ride. On rough roads it was well controlled and fairly competent. But someone at the Porsche engineering department plugged the

Tasteful American advertising from 1976.

PORSCHE

A NEW [PORS]CHE

924

One look at the new Porsche 924 and you'll realize this is no ordinary automobile.

The dynamic design of its clean, flowing lines instantly proclaims it to be unlike any other car you've ever seen.

Here is a perfect blending of the designer's search for beauty and the engineer's desire for efficiency. The shape of the new Porsche 924 not only pleases the eye, but it slices the wind so cleanly that it registered an incredibly low 0.36 drag coefficient in wind tunnel testing.

But the true innovativeness of this new Porsche lies much deeper than the sheet metal. It lies at the very heart of the car in a unique arrangement of the engine, clutch, and transmission, known as a "transaxle" system.

In this transaxle arrangement, the engine, a water-cooled overhead cam design with a continuous fuel injection system, is mounted in front. The clutch is placed directly behind it, giving quick, positive clutch action for rapid shifting.

The transmission, however, is mounted in the rear, at the driving wheels (hence the name rear "transaxle"). Rather than a conventional, heavy drive shaft with universal joints, there is a solid drive shaft in a hollow torque tube connecting the front-mounted engine with the rear-mounted transaxle. Thus, the entire drive train and differential is a single rigid unit which does away with universal joints and allows for more direct power transfer. Response is virtually instant. In addition, the gearshift is mounted directly on the torque tube, providing a short, precise throw.

But this unique transaxle system yields more than preciseness. It also results in an almost perfect 50-50 weight distribution which improves braking efficiency and enhances handling characteristics. The new Porsche 924 takes corners smoothly, in balance. McPherson struts in front, combined with a wishbone torsion bar suspension in the rear, keep body lean to a minimum in curves. Rack-and-pinion steering assures the driver of quick, accurate response to every command. The new Porsche 924 is designed to be the most driveable Porsche ever.

The new Porsche 924 is not inexpensive. But it is less than you'd expect to pay for a Porsche.

Another early piece of Stateside advertising. In the early years, adverts for the new Porsche appeared in enthusiast publications with monotonous regularity.

destined for the American market had slightly bigger aluminium bumpers mounted on energy-absorbing struts, and larger rubber inserts at the front leading to deletion of the driving lamps found on European models; as a result, overall length was 4320mm for US specification models. The cars also came with the obligatory side reflectors – an orange one between the front bumper and the wheelarch, and a red one mounted on the rear flanks close to the rear lights.

The most frequently used adjective for the car's interior was "functional" – Road Test even went as far as to say it was "a little Spartan for our tastes." There was nothing particularly pretty about it but, in typically German style, it did everything it was supposed to in a thoroughly efficient manner.

However, most testers praised the "intelligent design" of the seating and instrumentation and, after the 914, the practicality of the hatchback arrangement with its convenient glass panel, although some noted that the latter tended to slightly distort rearview vision; heating and ventilation was no more than average, with too little ram pressure to be comfortable without the fan in operation.

Road & Track carried out a comparison test between the 924, the two-litre Alfa Romeo Alfetta GT (GTV in Europe) and Datsun's 280Z. Despite qualms about the ride and the rather high price, the well-built Stuttgart machine came out an easy winner. "No doubt this is only the first of many victories for the 924," the magazine said. "Perhaps some day

wrong number into a computer because the freeway ride is about the worst we have experienced." The *Motor Trend* test echoed this last observation, concluding "the impression is that you can take a chuckhole in stride, but hit a matchstick and you'll know it instantly."

Steering and brakes were considered well above average by most, but the old criticisms regarding unexpectedly poor levels of NVH control would not go away. Porsche acknowledged that there was a regrettable anomaly, and promised "revised suspension tuning to either reduce or eliminate the problem" for future production cars heading across the Atlantic.

As for styling, Road Test remarked "they should have no trouble selling it, if only on looks alone. Most of the comments indicated a genuine approval of the 924's shape." 924s

Standard coachwork colours (1977 MY)
Black, Rallye Yellow, Scarlet, Signal Green, Brocade Red, Polar White.

Special coachwork colours
Copper Metallic, Turquoise, Bahama Blue Metallic, Reseda Green Metallic, Diamond Silver Metallic.

Trim materials
Black or Gazelle leatherette with matching inlays. Alternatively, inlays could be in Saddle Brown, Black/
Yellow or Black/Silver Tartan Dress cloth. Carpets came in Black or Gazelle (a tan colour).

even the Porsche fanatics will come out of their ivory tower and learn to love the 924."

A British viewpoint

Although the 924 appeared in a number of publications during the latter part of 1975 and had been displayed in rhd form at the 1976 Earls Court Show, it wasn't until February 1977 that the car went on sale in the UK. By this time, side rubbing strips were a feature and a more useful voltmeter had replaced the oil temperature gauge (a throwback from air cooling days).

The promised automatic gearbox was available shortly after as a £450 option. As such, the 924 became the first Porsche to offer a fully-automatic transmission, as opposed to a semi-automatic one. This was also sourced from Audi (the Type O-87). However, unlike the manual cars where the clutch was attached to the engine, with the three-speed automatic, the torque converter went to the rear bell-housing, making the front one superfluous. With a 3.44:1 final drive, it added a good couple of seconds to the 0-60 time, but most of the 924s sold in the UK were equipped with manual transmission.

Motor was one of the first magazines to test the latest Porsche, covering it in the issue dated 19 February. Having remarked on the relatively light weight of the vehicle and its slippery aerodynamic form, its report stated:

This roll-out blind was a useful standard feature fitted to cars for all markets from August 1976.

A European specification car for the 1977 model year. Note the side rubbing strips and new-style badging; both were adopted for all markets from this point.

"Performance is excellent, especially considering the engine capacity, yet economy has not suffered ... The 924 is a sports car in the modern idiom, achieving much through efficiency rather than brute force."

The magazine thought the engine was rather noisy at high revs, but conceded that the unit was turning over at only 3400rpm at 70mph (the UK motorway speed limit), and at this cruising speed it was "relatively unobtrusive." Starting was said to be "instant, whatever the weather" and the engine pulled "cleanly if not strongly from low revs before the water temperature gauge needle had moved from its stop." All of these observations were confirmed during my period of 924 ownership (it was a five-speed 1978 example), even after the car had clocked up an intergalactic 150,000 miles.

Motor felt the gear ratios were "ideal" and, in contrast to the Alfetta tested, found the synchromesh "unbeatable. However, reverse is too close to first, and the detents are not really strong enough to differentiate clearly between the two gears." On the four-speed 'box (all that was available at the time of the test, at least as far as manual transmissions were concerned), first to fourth gears were arranged in a traditional 'H' pattern, with reverse at top left opposite first.

The front seats offered "plenty of support in all the most important areas" and were described as firm but very comfortable, while the steering was "very much like that of the 911, for it is light at anything above walking pace, and writhes gently in your hands, telling you exactly what the front wheels are doing: it is full of feel, precise and responsive – just as a good steering system should be." Once again, though, it was pointed out that either the steering wheel was too low or the seats too high, as the driver's hands tended to foul on the thighs during sharp cornering manoeuvres.

Handling was said to be "nicely neutral and progressive, but on the limit it can be a little unpredictable," while the ride was described as "typical Porsche in that [it] has to some extent been sacrificed for good, taut handling."

However, the familiar complaints about low-speed ride quality were omnipresent, as were comments about poor bump-thump suppression. It seems that the Americans were not alone in encountering this problem, either.

The sad thing is that this, combined with wind noise (something a few magazines thought excessive, although it must be said that just as many commented on the low level of wind noise), and far from silky engine performance made many feel that the 924 lacked refinement, especially in view of its hefty price tag.

Fortunately, the brakes received almost unilateral praise. It should be noted, however, that *Motor Sport* found them "a trifle spongy and over-servoed, though providing good stopping power until this Porsche was punished very hard, then some fade was obvious."

Motor testers applauded the speed and positive action of the pop-up headlight mechanism, but even though the car came with 60/55W Halogen bulbs, *Motor* – in contrast to the *Motor Sport* report – was not overly impressed by their performance and added "the driving lights didn't seem to make much difference."

Motor also had a problem with the fact that the wipers were not converted to better suit rhd vehicles, and were none too pleased that the owner had to pay for a rear wiper on such an expensive machine. "Sparsely equipped" seemed to sum up what most felt.

At the end of the *Motor* road test, a top speed of 121mph was recorded (though quite confident that Porsche's claimed 125mph was easily attainable in the right conditions), a very respectable 0-60 time of 8.2 seconds, and a 17.0 standing-quarter – terminal speed, 87mph. All of this while returning an average of 25.5mpg over 1200 hard-driven miles was highly commendable, and put the 924 near the top of its class.

For comparison, it is interesting to look at the figures recorded by *Autocar* in a sister car: a top speed of 126mph, 0-60mph in 9.7 seconds (a long way off the *Motor* time), and a standing-quarter just 0.2 seconds different;

The 'Celebration' model, seen here in US trim.

fuel consumption averaged out at a brilliant 27.8mpg.

Although *Motor Sport* described the new Porsche as "a disappointment," most testers from enthusiast publications came away with a good overall impression of the car. *Autocar* said it had "excellent economy, handling, ride, braking, and adequate performance," for instance.

However, the poor exchange meant a list price far higher than would be

ideal. At the time of its introduction, a basic 924 cost £6999, with options such as alloy wheels with wider 185/70 section tyres at £264, anti-roll bars at £81, headlight washers at £78, a leather-trimmed steering wheel at £44, not to mention the £248 sunroof, metallic paint at £230, tinted glass at £98, stereo equipment, and so on, leaving the latest Porsche model at a distinct disadvantage when it was compared to some of its major rivals.

The Alfa Romeo GTV was listed at just £4999. As far as the author is concerned, in many ways it was the better car, offering the same thoroughbred pedigree and what felt like superior performance, even if the figures on paper said otherwise – the five-speed gearbox and low-down torque doubtless helped. The biggest minus points were doubtful reliability (especially compared to the bulletproof Porsche), nowhere near the same level of fit and finish, and Alfa's notorious rust problem during that period. To pinch a favourite quote from an old test report on the Maserati Biturbo, the Milanese beauty was perhaps best left to "brave eccentrics" – and yes, before you ask, I had one of those (a 222E coupé), too!

The two-litre Lancia HPE was another Italian model worth looking at, especially at the price, being even cheaper than the Alfa, but offering a more than respectable turn of speed. Others to consider included the Reliant Scimitar GTE (decent performance, practical, no rust problems and a good buy at £5480), the well-equipped and powerful Datsun 260Z 2+2 (which offered a saving of £500 on the basic 924), and the Saab 99 EMS or TVR 3000M for those who wanted something a little different from the evergreen but somewhat stereotypical Ford Capri.

Going up the price range (which most 924 owners would, as in reality very few would be able to specify a completely basic car even if they wanted one), for £8200 one could secure a Jaguar XJ4.2C – high

71

Right: The second member of the Porsche transaxle family – the 928. Rather than competing in the two-litre class, this luxury model was designed to take on the likes of the Jaguar XJ-S and Mercedes 450SLC.

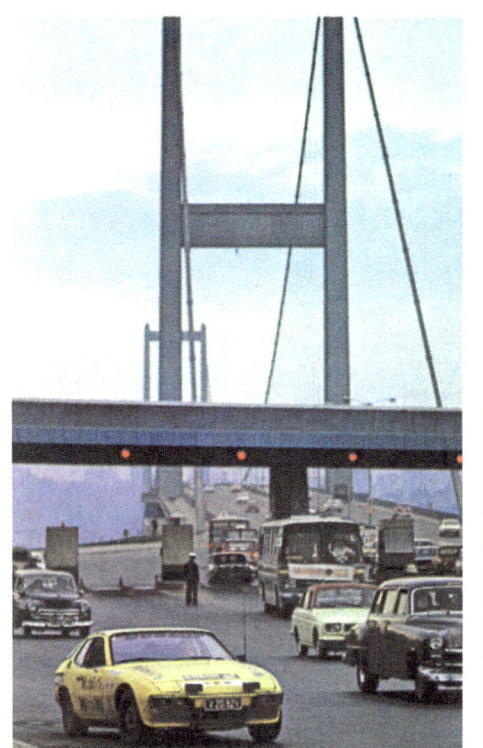

Rudi Lins and Gerhard Plattner on their way around the world.

A 1977.5 model year Porsche 924 for the US market, which incorporated a number of engine and detail improvements. Note the heavy bumpers necessary to comply with Federal regulations.

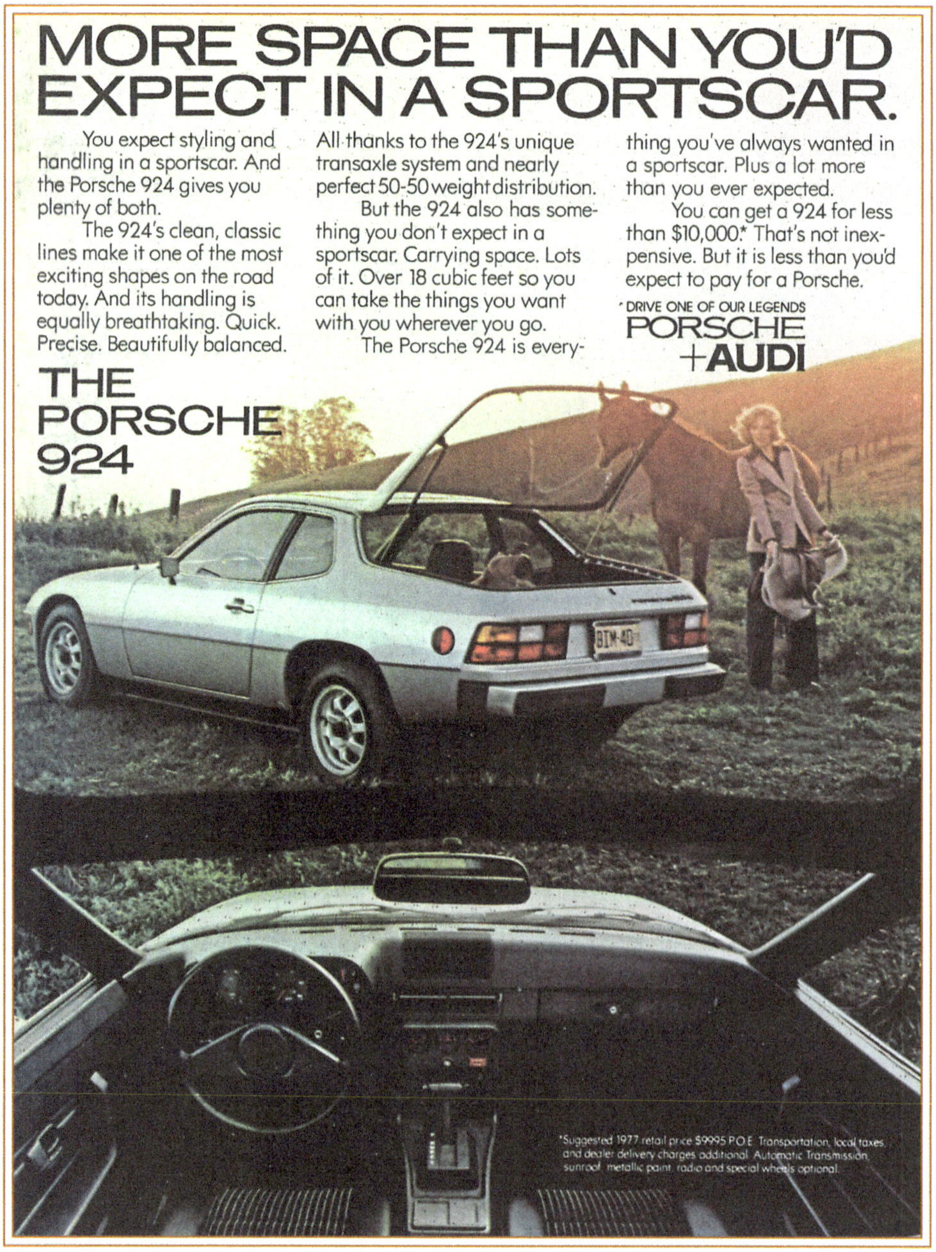

fuel consumption, but excellent performance combined with true luxury at a snip. As for the Lotus Elite, Eclat and the new Esprit, I'm not sure they could be classed as bargains, but they offered a very competitive package if one looked at them from an angle of all-round performance for the money. Personally, with the latter marque, I would have gone for the Stuttgart machine, but there can be no doubt that Lotus had a lot to offer and a strong following, its image enhanced by the company's F1 involvement at that time.

On the subject of boosting images through motorsport endeavours, not long after the 924's UK introduction, Porsche produced 3000 'Celebration' models to commemorate the company's victory in the World Sportscar Championship – 924s finished in Grand Prix White with the famous Martini red, blue and black stripes (a similar scheme was offered on the contemporary 911 Turbo). The limited

edition car also came equipped with white-painted alloy wheels, front and rear anti-roll bars, a sunroof, special red and black interior trim, and a leather-covered steering wheel. Only 100 were sent to the UK (priced at £7673), as 2000 of them went to the States. I remember being offered one of these in mint condition during the late-1980s, and I'm still kicking myself for turning it down.

Endurance runs

Austrian Porsche enthusiasts, Rudi Lins and Gerhard Plattner, took an early production 924 on a 6000 mile run from Austria to Finland in the closing days of 1975. This, an achievement in itself given the weather conditions, was simply intended as a trial run for a marathon trip around the world.

Sponsored by Bosch, Mobil and the Austrian Tourism Board, and starting out from Innsbruck on 23 April 1976, they returned 28 days later, having crossed five Continents and completed no less than 13,865 miles along the way. A shock absorber had to be replaced, but otherwise the yellow 924 was untouched for the entire jaunt.

In addition to running non-stop for 100 hours on the Brenner autobahn, a second journey less than a year later saw the intrepid pair travel from Hammerfest, the northernmost town in the world, through Europe, and on to South America to visit the southernmost town, Ushuaia in Argentina: in other words, the North Cape to Cape Horn. After 20,500 miles in extreme temperatures, the only parts that needed replacing en route were a damaged shock and a leaking fuel filter.

These endurance runs were later used in Porsche advertising material – and why not? The 924 used was the same one for the autobahn record-breaking run and both excursions around the world! In over 40,000 miles, the vehicle had run faultlessly; two broken shock absorbers (one following a particularly heavy landing on rough roads and another after dropping into a pothole at high speed) were the only real problems experienced. This was indeed an excellent display of reliability.

The 928

Introduced in February 1977, the 928 made its public debut at the following month's Geneva Show. It was a member of the same family as the 924, with a front-mounted, water-cooled engine and transaxle to give good weight distribution. The engine, in this instance, however, was a V8 unit of 4.5 litres designed to tempt customers who traditionally bought from Jaguar and Mercedes-Benz. The brainchild of Dr Fuhrmann, it was immediately voted 'Car of the Year'.

In actual fact, work on the 928 had started before the 924 project, as at one point it was put forward as the possible successor to the 911 range. However, when the Type 924 passed to Porsche ownership, because the need for a cheaper car was greater, it was the smaller model that was developed first.

The 928, being a luxury Grand Tourer, was not cheap by any standards. In America, its largest market, it cost $28,500 on introduction. This compares to $11,995 for a 924, or $19,500 for a 911SC coupé – only the 911 Turbo was more expensive. The 155mph 928S was added to the range in August 1979, with the engine bored out to give 4.7 litres and 300bhp.

924 developments

Following a number of reports of fuel vapourisation, the fuel pump was

The automatic gearbox opened up the 924 to a wider audience, especially in North America and Japan. Note the air conditioning switch situated where the clock would usually be (with air conditioning, the clock was moved over to the right, and the voltmeter done away with).

relocated to a cooler area under the right-hand rear wing, and after the first 20 rhd cars had been built, all those that followed were fitted with a modified throttle linkage, because it was found that if the bonnet was slammed shut, the original linkage was just high enough to dent the panel (these engines were known by the XJ designation).

Porsche also recommended that for those particularly sensitive to road noise, the OE (original equipment) steel-braced Uniroyal radials could be replaced with Pirelli CN36 tyres at a suitable point in time, although the engineers were already working on a much better solution. Interestingly, most road tests conducted during 1977 featured Dunlop SP Sport tyres, at least when the wider 185/70 HR14 items were fitted.

Meanwhile, cars destined for American shores had been substantially improved by February 1977. Designated as 1977.5 MY models, the latest 924 featured more power, a different final-drive ratio and a number of other refinements. The engine received modified pistons (allowing an increase in the compression ratio – now 8.5:1 instead

of the former 8.0:1), bigger inlet valves (the latest items were 40mm diameter as opposed to the 38mm diameter originally specified), and revised camshaft and ignition timing. All cars now came with a catalytic converter to curb emissions, while Californian specification models also featured air injection.

The worthwhile result was 110bhp at 5750rpm (an increase of 15bhp), although the gain in torque was a negligible 2lbft, developed 500rpm higher up the rev range than before. However, although the additional power was very welcome, that wasn't the end of the story, as the modifications

improved engine response and flexibility, and also enhanced the unit's high rpm refinement: despite the hike in compression, 91 octane grade unleaded fuel could still be used. The 49-State engines carried the XG designation, while California (and Japan) versions were given the XE appellation.

As noted earlier, the US specification cars also received a new final-drive ratio. In place of the original 3.44:1, a lower 3.88:1 ratio was fitted, bringing about an improvement in low- and mid-range acceleration. Oddly and despite the lower ratio – because of the engine's new-found willingness to approach the 6500rpm red line in fourth gear, top speed was actually higher than before, with 117mph being recorded by *Road & Track*. As one would expect, maximum speeds in the other three gears fell slightly, but the quarter-mile could now be dismissed in 18 seconds dead with a terminal speed of 77mph.

"Another welcome improvement is

Driver's view of the various gearboxes on offer during 1978. From left to right: the Audi four-speed manual, Porsche five-speed manual and Audi three-speed automatic. A leather gaiter was fitted to the gearlever from early 1978.

British advertising from the 1978 model year. The Lux basically replaced the 'Celebration' model.

wheels with 185/70 HR14 tyres, three speakers, an aerial and suppression kit for $345. The Group II option batched together headlight washers, and front and rear anti-roll bars.

Individual options included air conditioning at $548, the removable roof panel (very reasonable at just $330), metallic paint ($295), an AM/FM radio ($135) and anti-roll bars at $105. Another important option, especially in the States where the majority of people prefer to not have the hassle of shifting gears, was the three-speed automatic transmission unit (the ratios being 2.55:1 on first, 1.45:1 on second, and a direct top); with a slightly higher 3.73:1 final-drive, it cost $399, and was available from March.

Despite certain reservations from the motoring press, the car was an instant hit in the States, accounting for over 4500 sales in 1976 and more than 13,500 of the 20,000 Porsches sold in America during the following year.

The 1978 model year

In the UK, the Lux package was soon put together, and was available from August 1977. In reality, it was to become pretty much the standard model for the British market, as very few 'basic' cars were ever sold; with a healthy demand for the four-cylinder model, why sell the cheaper version! The eight-spoke alloy wheels previously offered as an option (complete with wider 185/70 HR14 tyres), now came as part of the Lux specification, along with convenience features such as tinted glass, a rear wiper and headlight washers.

the car's ride, which we called jouncy in our 1976 road test," said *Road & Track*. "At the time we suggested some retuning of the shock absorbers and torsion bars to alleviate this condition. But Porsche did it their way by tightening up quality control and narrowing the tolerances for installation of the transaxle and drivetrain in the body. Simple and seemingly effective." Although it felt the ride was still a fraction on the stiff side, *Motor Trend* was also satisfied, noting that "the oscillation has gone

and the car is now considerably more comfortable."

Sadly, the list price had already increased by some $600, which only served to highlight the same old niggling problems of a steering wheel that was mounted too low, and far too much noise for a $10,000 automobile. However, *Road & Track* felt the 924 was still an appealing machine, even at that price.

Options changed a little – the Group I package consisted of alloy

European lhd interior with the five-speed gearbox. Note the voltmeter on the right of the centre console, and the new Herringbone cloth seat inlays, replacing the rather dated Tartan.

The rear seats really were quite small, but fine for children or occasional adult use.

During mid-1977, journalist Clive Richardson had observed that the engine's "flat torque characteristics can't mask the massive gap between second and third gears. This ruins the charm of the car, which cries out for a five-speed gearbox."

In keeping with Porsche tradition for continual development, for the 1978 model year (introduced at the Frankfurt Show in September 1977), a Porsche-designed, five-speed gearbox was made available as a cost option, while the rear suspension mountings and exhaust system were modified. Different brake pad material prolonged life, measures were taken to improve hot starting, and the rear seat was now trimmed to match that of the front pair.

The Getrag five-speed gearbox was derived from a Porsche 911 unit, with first on a dog-leg opposite reverse,

and the upper four gears arranged in a traditional 'H' pattern. The additional cog allowed better spacing of the ratios, enabling the driver to make the most of the engine's fairly modest torque – the ratios being 2.79:1 on first, 1.72:1 on second, 1.22:1 on third, a slightly overdriven 0.93:1 on fourth and 0.71:1 on fifth, although with a 4.71:1 final-

drive, the overall gearing in top was the same.

The Type 016 five-speed transmission gave the desired effect of making the car feel livelier and more responsive, although the same overall gearing – combined with the temptation to use the gears more – actually increased fuel consumption.

American advertising for the 1978 model year.

Still, the *Autocar* recorded an average of 25.0mpg over 800 miles, which was easily a class-leading figure.

As for performance, although the 0-60 time went up, this could be explained by the fact that second gear ran out at 56mph, so another change was necessary (it was much the same situation with the Alfa GTV). In reality, the car, which weighed in at 2450lbs (1114kg) in Lux trim, was much better in everyday situations, and that was what mattered most; the standing-quarter could be accomplished in 17.1

The 1978 model year cars got a new exhaust system, identified by the oval-shaped tailpipe; it provided the 924 with better noise suppression and improved appearance. The familiar alloys were now available with black-painted centres, going some way towards aping those of the 911.

seconds, incidentally, whilst top speed was 126mph.

A November 1977 article in *Classic Cars* noted: "For the front-engined 924, changes are both engineering and cosmetic. The 1978 models are now quieter and brake pad life has been increased, while anti-roll bars are fitted at both ends for the British market; pile carpet is now used and the rear seats are cloth-trimmed. The 924 now costs £7350 with the 924

Lux, which incorporates a number of previous options – sports wheels, tinted windows, rear wiper and headlamp washers – coming out at £7800." Nonetheless, even in Lux guise, one still had to pay extra for a stereo and aerial, and automatic transmission (rare in the UK it has to be said) added another £429.

The rear suspension was now rubber-mounted and combined with better sound insulation. Even though there was a marked improvement, it was still far from perfect, according to some magazines. The Autocar stated: "It must be said that despite modifications to the suspension mountings, the 924 still suffers from suspension noise and bump-thump at low speeds when the ride is quite harsh and firm." However, it added that "at speed, the ride smooths out and is an excellent compromise between comfort and tautness."

The author has the greatest respect for the opinions of Bill Boddy, as they are always refreshingly honest and uncompromising, no matter what badge happens to adorn the bonnet. As the long-serving Editor of Motor Sport, he said of the 924: "It is a splendid car to drive, on account of very good handling, light steering with a generous lock, and spongy but powerful, progressive disc/drum braking. But it is certainly not like Porsches of old! For one thing, a stubby gearlever with its massive knob controls a nice change, if the movements are unhurried, but this isn't the famous Porsche synchromesh I used to know."

Boddy was actually testing a four-speed model, which didn't have the Porsche synchros – obviously no-one had told him, but one can also conclude that the difference between the Audi cone-type synchromesh and Porsche's rather more expensive ring-type synchro was quite noticeable.

After denouncing the oval-shaped steering wheel (which, according to him, failed in its main purpose of making it easier to see the instruments), Bill Boddy continued: "The suspension is on the hard side, the cornering exhibits very slight understeer, if full lock is required the steering feels to go 'over-centre' as it were, but normally castor-return action is good. The steering is at times a bit twitchy but very 'quick' and accurate. An individualistic feature is a right-hand handbrake lever, sensibly located, however.

"The front seats are very comfortable and the rear seats fold away. I regard the 924's rear compartment, however, as a claustrophobic cavern, making it really a sports two-seater. The front seat head restraints add to this feeling."

The 924 was very economical, returning an average of 29.1mpg, but he concluded that, in spite of the car's high gearing, "there is still a good deal of exhaust noise, nor is tyre thump absent. The engine fluffed unless it was running at over 2000rpm. So this is a car for the more enthusiastic to drive properly, which its exceptionally likeable handling endorses. One really needs the optional five-speed gearbox."

Regarding the five-speed transmission, which could be supplied with an optional limited-slip differential according to the catalogue, the *Autocar* noted: "The change itself is one that has to be mastered, but bearing in mind the length of the linkage running to the gearbox, it is of very high quality once learnt." This view was echoed by a friend of the author's, who struggled with the dog-leg first and narrow gate in my old car, whereas after several thousand miles, the unusual gearchange layout became second nature.

Although the baby Porsche certainly had its fans and critics in seemingly equal numbers, writing for *Classic Cars*, Michael Bowler noted that the 924 "is solidly built, fast, economical, practical and a pleasure to drive whatever the conditions." In reality, what more could one ask of the car?

1978 Stateside

The Clean Air Act in the US was putting more and more pressure on car makers to cut emissions, but asked for too much, too soon. Indeed, when the 1978 regulations were announced, there was a distinct possibility that there would be no more Porsches for America. The Stuttgart marque was not on its own, however, as most manufacturers stated that there was no way they could make their vehicles comply. Fortunately, the bill wasn't passed, but it was nonetheless a very worrying time for the factory and enthusiasts alike.

The five-speed gearbox became an option for the 1978 model year, but used a 5.00:1 final-drive ratio in the US. The list price had shot up to $11,995 (for 1979, it would increase again, this time by more than $2600). Option prices had also gone up, but somehow the 924 remained as popular as ever – 10,433 were sold in the States during 1978.

By now, the entire bodyshell was being hot-dip galvanised, and offered in the colours shown in the table on page 78.

Throughout 1978, the factory produced a number of special editions – M426 (the same number allocated to the 'Celebration' model) was a Dolomite Grey Metallic car, as was M427. However, the former was only available in the States (limited to 1800 units), whilst the latter was a run of 100 vehicles for the French market. There were also 100 cars for Switzerland, finished in Pearl Metallic.

Other 924 specials

On April 24, 1978, the 50,000th 924 left the NSU works. The 924 was already in service with the German Police Force, and that month the Notarzt 924 – a fast response vehicle that allowed doctors to reach medical emergencies in the shortest possible time – made its debut at the Wiesbaden Medical Congress. With two roof-mounted lights and additional horns, it came with a carphone, two-way radio, a medical bag, ECG equipment and a defibrillator.

The rumour mill was suggesting a five-cylinder Targa version of the 924 for 1978, but, if it existed at all, it was destined never to appear in public. It's quite a shame, actually, as this would have made an interesting project. However, a number of outside companies, such as Morse in America, were quick to offer soft-top conversions on the 924. Perhaps the strangest custom body came from the workshops of Gunther Artz of Hannover, who built shooting brakes on both the 924 and 928.

Giving the 924 more 'go' was by far the most popular type of conversion, though. BAE of California had a bolt-on turbocharger kit on the market within weeks of the 924 arriving in the States. Within three years, BAE had sold more than 1000 packages to those drivers who sought a little extra excitement from their new prize possession. The BAE modification provided 155bhp and a standing-quarter time of just over 17 seconds. By 1980, the price was around $1200 for a kit, or $1600 fitted – quite reasonable prices when one considers the worthwhile jump in horsepower and torque, and the corresponding improvement in on-the-road performance.

Perhaps the best-known of the aftermarket turbo conversions came from the Windblown concern of New York, which not only developed systems for Porsches, but Volkswagens, BMWs and Fiats as well (indeed, Fiat's American arm asked Windblown to produce a turbo installation for the 124 Spider, which was then sold through official channels). The respected journalist, John Dinkel, described the Windblown 924 as "the most flexible, most driveable and nicest running turbocharged car – production or aftermarket – I have ever driven." For

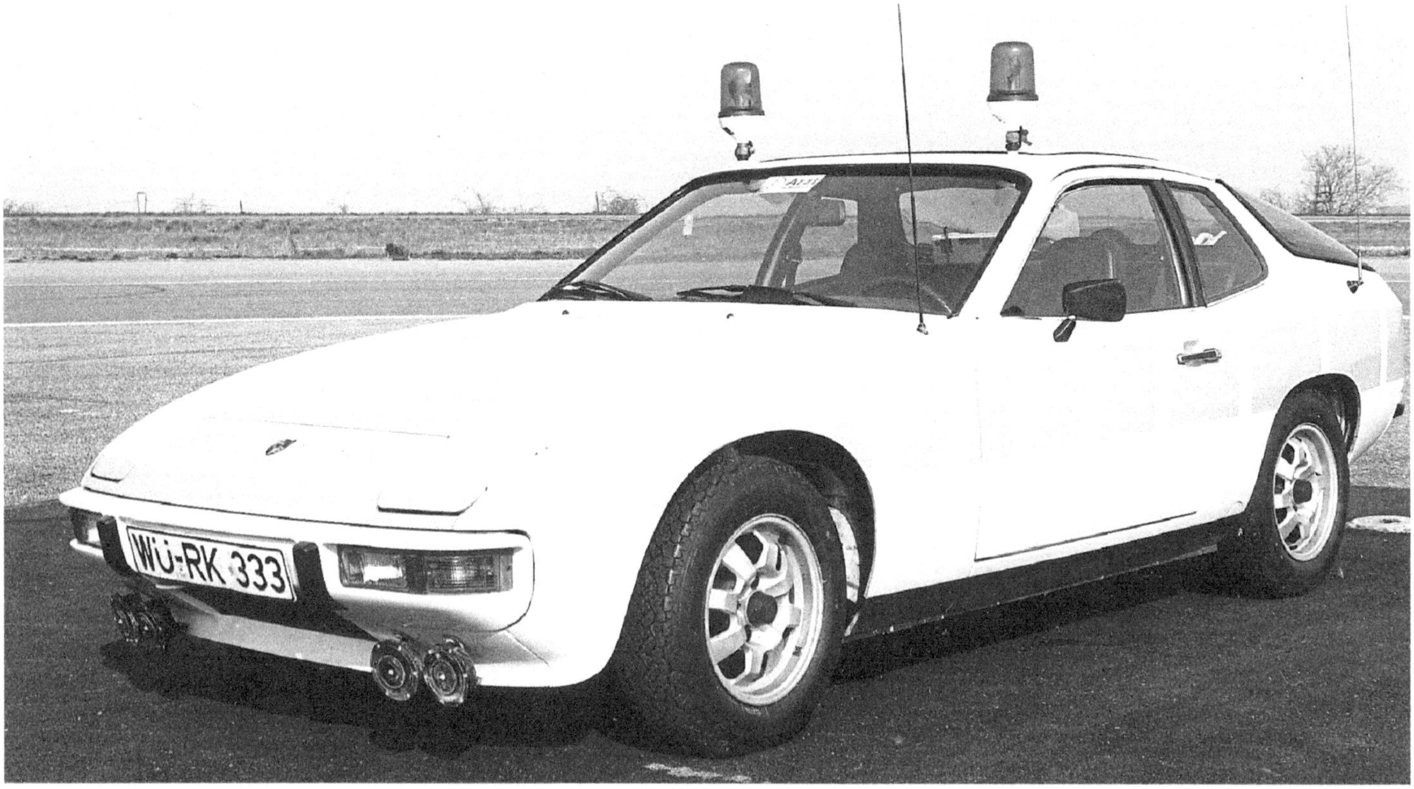
WÜ-RK 333

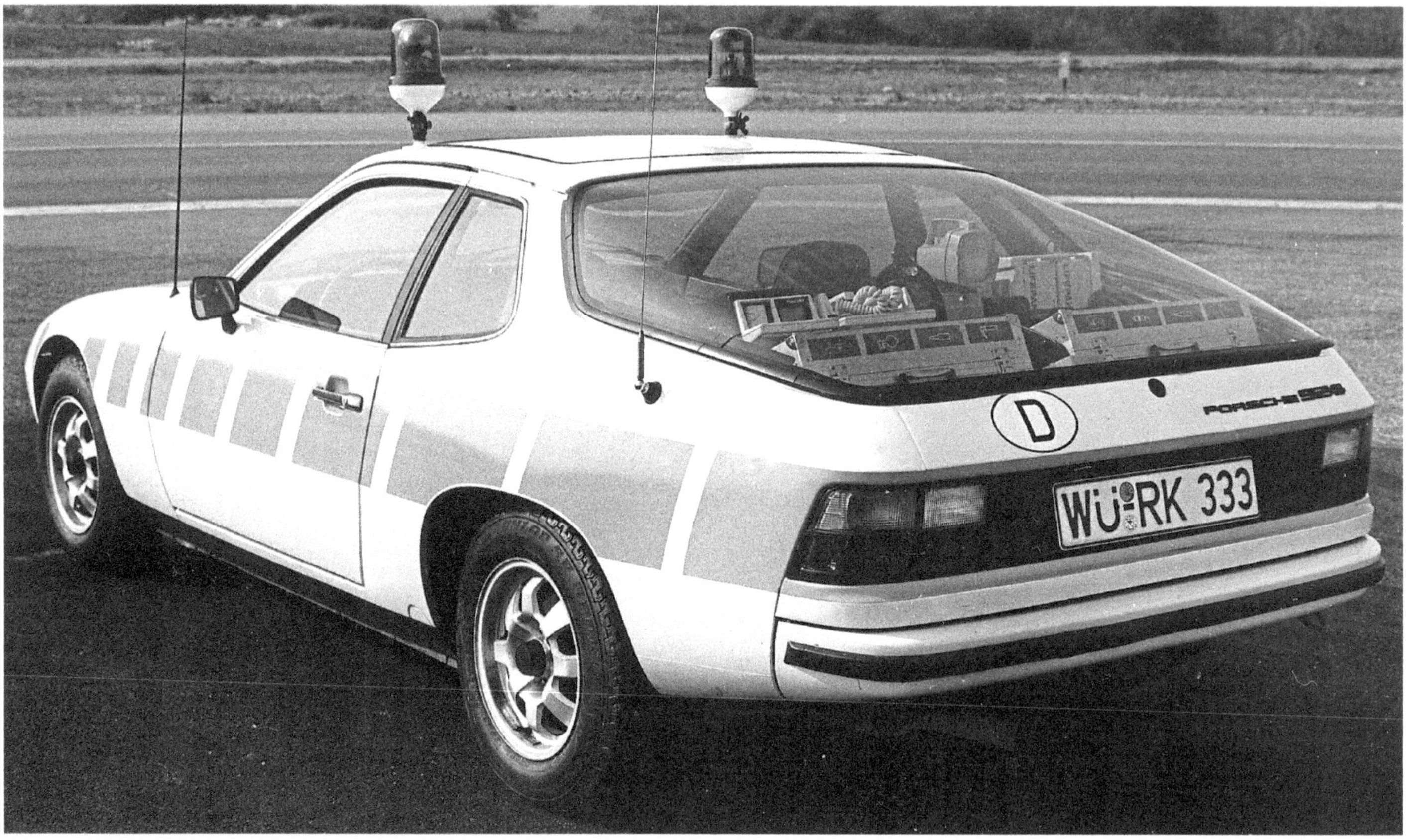
D
PORSCHE 924
WÜ-RK 333

The Notarzt 924, introduced at the 1978 Wiesbaden Medical Congress, was a fast response vehicle for doctors.

As well as investigating supercharging the 924 to give better performance, Porsche engineers also looked into running the model on methanol fuel to as it was more environmentally-friendly. Nothing came of either of these worthy projects.

Left, above: A 924 Police car. The factory also produced some far less conspicuous vehicles for the German Police Force, identified only by a bank of sirens where the front number plate would usually be.

Left, below: Rear view of the German Police car.

Its export market price tag meant that the 924 was certainly not a "poor man's Porsche" as some had dubbed it. It didn't deserve that cruel label in any case as it had blossomed into a nice car, worthy of the famous badge. By 1978, however, the model had reached a crossroads, and was about to take the route signposted performance.

just over $2000, the buyer received a very comprehensive kit, and a transformed 924 – a car now capable of covering the standing-quarter in 15.3 seconds and 0-60 in under seven seconds.

A number of others also offered turbocharger kits, while John Butera of California (an experienced drag car builder) provided a highly-developed supercharger kit. Although it cost around $1400 in 1979, it cut the 0-60 time down to just 7.7 seconds, with the supercharger offering instant response throughout the rev range – a strong advantage over a turbocharger with its inherent lag as it shifts from being off boost to coming on boost.

Porsche is known to have tried supercharging the 924 itself (the project was allocated the Type 931 designation and the engine given the 047 appellation) but, sadly, nothing came of it; supercharging was considered decidedly old-fashioned once the turbo era was in full swing. It is interesting to note that, as the 1990s drew to a close, several manufacturers had begun to market supercharged models, this gentlemanly form of forced induction at last making a comeback.

Matters of the moment

The German magazine, *Auto Motor und Sport*, had overwhelmingly voted the 924 the 'Best Sports Car' in the under two-litre class for 1977 and '78, but prices were rising apparently out of control. To be fair, it wasn't exactly Porsche's fault – exchange rates were not in the company's favour. However,

the bottom line was that the 924 was becoming decidedly expensive in export markets, and Ferry Porsche later stated that "if we had been able to cut the price by 20%, it would have found its proper niche in the market."

By August 1978, the 924 Lux was a hefty £8299, although the Lux package now included electric windows, and an electrically-adjustable heated driver's door mirror for the 1979 model year (both had become options for 1978). With most people opting for the five-speed gearbox (an additional £365) and the removable sunroof (a further £241), the choice between a top specification 924 or two Ford Capri 3000Ss for the same money was ridiculous, especially in view of its no better than average performance. The Datsun 260Z 2+2 could match the Stuttgart machine in most departments, and was certainly a lot better equipped for less than £7000; then there was the Alfa Romeo GTV, £1000 cheaper again!

The *Autocar* noted at the time that "the 924's price pushes it almost up to the bottom of the supercar bracket, exemplified by the Lotus Eclat 521 [then £10,475] with its ultimate standards of performance and roadholding. At the other end of the scale, the Ford Capri 3000S [at £4595] does pretty much the same job as the 924 for little more than half the price ... One is, unfortunately, paying a good deal for that prestigious hallmark."

In America, *Road & Track* carried out a comparison test with four automatic coupés – the 924 (listed at $14,600), Datsun's 280ZX ($9899), the Chevrolet

Corvette ($10,220), and the recently-introduced Mazda RX-7 ($7995 in GS guise). The Stuttgart machine didn't come out of it too well. The magazine concluded that "the Porsche 924 offers the best handling of the lot, a crisp Teutonic line and a sort of understated Olde Worlde quality. But its lackluster performance adds insult to injury by suggesting that someone pay $18,000 [with options] just to be humiliated on the highway."

In another article, John Dinkel, writing for the same magazine in the April 1979 issue, noted the following: "You might think R&T is starting to sound like a broken record, but damn it, we're frustrated. The cause of that frustration? Porsche's 924. On paper it has all the makings of a great GT. In truth, the steering, handling, interior layout, seating, instrumentation and styling are all in the Porsche tradition. And we must admit that evolutionary improvements have alleviated a few of the niggling problems that have plagued the 924 since it was introduced in 1976 (especially a classic case of freeway hoppus Californium). This brings us to the reason of our discontent: the engine. The Audi-designed two-litre is noisy, rough and buzzy and, adding injury to insult, gives performance hardly commensurate with a GT of the 924's supposed stature and price – now up to $14,600."

Fortunately, Porsche had something up its sleeve. As Chairman of the Management Committee and Director of Engineering since 1972, Dr Fuhrmann, naturally, played an important role in both the 924's origins

and its future course. In 1976, he promised: "Under our guidance, the 924 will develop like a real Porsche." Its chassis certainly had plenty of scope for further development, and, thanks to an elegant, timeless body shape, the engineers at Weissach didn't have to rush it. Unlike the 914, the 924 was not going to date quickly, so it could mature and become ever more competent over a number of years, rather like the 911 had before it.

At last, just as the critics were starting to gang up on the 924, the first major development on the model since its introduction silenced them all in one stunning blow – enter the 924 Turbo.

4

THE 924 TURBO

As mentioned in the previous chapter, Porsche had looked into the idea of equipping the 924 with a supercharger, but, apart from the ill-fated Cisitalia, most of the company's post-war experience with forced induction had come from turbocharging: Porsche's fearsome endurance racers had featured turbo power for some years, and the 911 Turbo (Type 930) launched a new road car era for the Stuttgart concern at the 1974 Paris Salon. A higher powered version of the 924 had always been envisaged by Porsche management, so it was only really a matter of time before they installed a turbo in the model.

The 928 had not been the sales success Fuhrmann had hoped for (not through any fault of the car, but due to world economy in general), and suggestions regarding a cheaper six-cylinder version were quickly dismissed as it simply defeated the object of the machine. Prototype 924s with turbochargers (two with larger turbos, and two with smaller items) had been spotted by the US press in summer 1978, so it came as no surprise when Porsche officially announced its plans. Would this be the way to ultimately replace the 911?

The 924 Turbo

As Fuhrmann had promised, the 924 was continually developed and, in response to demands for more power, in November 1978, three years after the new series first appeared, a 170bhp turbocharged version made its official debut. Overseen by Paul Hensler and designated the Type 931 (or 932 for rhd

models), the 924 Turbo helped redefine the modern sports car, combining thoroughbred progress with civility and comfort.

The K26 turbocharger was sourced from the KKK concern (Kuhnle, Kopp & Kausch), an exhaust-driven unit with a wastegate to limit boost to about 10psi and a circulating valve taken from the 911 Turbo. It was mounted low down on the exhaust side, the pressurised air being carried to the inlet manifold via a casting over the top of the engine. It was quite an elegant installation, with a '924 Turbo' badge on the aforementioned aluminium alloy pipe, and a 'Porsche' one atop the plenum chamber.

The engine's bottom end was deemed strong enough for it to continue unchanged. However, the alloy head was completely new. The sohc arrangement was retained, but there were redesigned combustion chambers with recessed valves (bigger 36mm diameter exhaust valves were incorporated at the same time), and the spark plugs (with platinum electrodes for the Turbo) were moved over to the intake side instead of the exhaust side, as in the normally-aspirated 924.

The Bosch K-Jetronic fuel-injection system was re-calibrated and the compression ratio lowered to 7.5:1 (it is normal practice to specify a lower c/r with turbocharged engines) through a combination of the new combustion chamber shape and different forged pistons, while an oil cooler was added to enable the engine to cope with the additional stresses imposed upon it. In addition, transistorised, breakerless electronic ignition was employed, along

The turbocharged version of the 924 engine weighed just 64lbs (29kg) more than its normally-aspirated counterpart, and as a result, weight distribution was hardly affected. Note the new position of the alternator, made necessary because of turbo location.

with a second fuel pump (both later adopted on normally-aspirated models) and a new sump.

With these modifications, the engine now developed 170bhp at 5500rpm and no less than 180lbft of torque at 3500rpm. This represented a 36% increase in horsepower, and a healthy 48% boost in maximum torque output. To take the extra power to the transaxle, the original 20mm diameter shaft was replaced by a beefier 25mm item needing only three support bearings.

While the five-speed manual transmission was still an option on the normally-aspirated 924, on the Turbo it came as standard, along with a larger diameter clutch (up from 215 to 225mm, and now hydraulically-operated instead of by cable). However, in typically thorough fashion, the gearbox mainshaft was strengthened, as were the differential and driveshafts.

The final-drive ratio was also changed, raised from 4.71:1 to 4.12:1 – as a result, the first gear was altered from 2.79:1 to 3.17:1 and second went from 1.72 to 1.78, doubtless to get the turbo kicking in as soon as possible, although the top three ratios remained the same; intermediate maxima through the gears was quoted as being 35, 62, 87 and 112mph respectively.

The semi-trailing arms at the rear were also uprated, as were the wheel hubs and bearings, the latter being sourced from the 911SC. This meant a five-stud wheel fitting, but due to the different offset compared to the 911, this subsequently led to two new alloy

Bodywork changes were kept to a minimum. Note the apertures in the nose, additional slats in the front spoiler, and the NACA duct on the bonnet. There was also a spoiler fixed to the rear hatch, and a new alloy wheel design. These early cars still had the VW Golf petrol cap showing, with the earliest models also carrying the chrome side window trim, although the latter was quickly changed to an all-black finish on the Turbo, becoming standard on all 924s for 1980.

wheel designs being adopted. Braking was now via Porsche ventilated discs all-round (283mm diameter at the front, 289mm at the rear), with the floating calipers coming off the 928.

Although stopping distances were reduced, the additional weight of the vehicle meant it was a negligible amount – the biggest advantage of the new set-up was the complete absence of fade, even after the toughest of testing sessions. The handbrake was now via drums built into the rear discs, a la 911, an arrangement which maintained a decent parking brake.

Naturally, given the enhanced performance capabilities of the Turbo, the suspension was uprated. Spring rates were altered, the standard Boge shock absorbers were replaced by

Koni units at the front and Bilsteins at the rear, and the anti-roll bars were changed – an increase to 23mm diameter at the front and a slimmer 14mm bar for the back. Ground clearance was unchanged, however.

The rear track was increased to 1390mm and the steering ratio was altered to give 3.8 turns lock-to-lock instead of four, by the use of longer steering arms. The standard cast alloy wheels were of a multi-spoke design, the 6J rims playing host to 185/70 VR15 tyres. Although not as attractive, smooth-looking 6J x 16 forged alloy wheels were promised for the future as an option, and these came fitted with VR-rated 205/55-section low-profile Pirelli P7 rubber.

Changes to the bodywork were

intentionally minimal: four apertures to direct air onto the oil cooler in the leading edge of the nose, a NACA duct on the bonnet to dissipate heat from around the turbo, further ventilation in the front airdam to provide additional brake cooling, and a neat polyurethane spoiler mounted on the rear hatch. The spoiler not only increased downforce, but also brought the coefficient of drag down from 0.36 for a standard 924 to just 0.34.

There were even fewer changes inside the car, which was something of a disappointment for some. The steering wheel was of a new, three-spoke design, however, borrowed from the 911SC. Although this was the same 380mm diameter as the original 924 two-spoke item, a 928-style four-

The Turbo was available to the home market from February 1979, with prices starting at DM39,480. By this time, around 63,000 normally-aspirated examples had been built.

spoke wheel could be specified with a 360mm outside diameter. New gauges, plus electric windows and electrically-adjustable door mirrors as standard, were further features, and turbocharged models brought back Tartan trim. This looks timeless and elegant inside a coat from Burberrys, but oh so seventies when used in a car interior.

Although it couldn't be seen, one big change in the cockpit was the noise – or rather the lack of it. The turbocharger absorbed some, and, combined with better sound insulation against road roar and under-bonnet noise, there was a marked improvement, and a number of contemporary reports commented on it. Indeed, at 60mph, the noise level in the original 924 was a quite raucous 74dB, whereas the turbocharged car was nearer 71dB. To put that into perspective, it was now almost on a par with its relatively quiet Japanese rivals from the same period. Another thing that couldn't be seen was a boost gauge, an item Porsche considered unnecessary, but most testers felt was a serious omission.

While a typical UK specification 924 weighed in at around 2485lbs (1130kg) at this time, the Turbo was only 110lbs (50kg) heavier. Needless to say, in turbocharged form, the 924's performance was transformed. According to factory figures, the 0-60 time was cut to just 7.8 seconds and the top speed shot up to 140mph. Just as impressive, fuel consumption was only about 20% down on that of the normally-aspirated car – a small price to pay for the lashings of extra horsepower and torque.

Left-hand drive production for the home market began in November 1978 at the rate of about 20 cars a day, with right-hand drive cars coming off the line the following summer. It is interesting to note that, unlike the standard 924 engines, which were entirely produced by Volkswagen, the turbocharged units were built up and tested in Porsche's own Zuffenhausen works.

Early press reaction

The press was duly invited to Friedrichshafen near the Swiss border to try the new model, at that time, the most powerful two-litre road car in the world. Clive Richardson, part-time racing driver (sometimes partnering my good friend, Win Percy) and a *Motor Sport* regular, wasn't overly impressed, but it's fair to say that, on this occasion, he was in the minority.

Writing for the *Autocar*, Tony Howard observed the following about the turbo installation: "The result is a mild-mannered car in which – either by accident or design – one is not particularly aware that it has a turbocharger at all ... On the whole, the turbocharger's impact on engine performance is very manageable. But, typical of this form of aspiration, acceleration feels notably flat, particularly if the revs are allowed to fall below 2000rpm. Full throttle from there produces no unpleasantness but little excitement until the 180lbft peak torque is reached at 3500rpm ... and the power curve starts to get away on its steep trajectory. From about 4000rpm upwards, the engine starts to pull hard, and acceleration is rapid – deceptively so because, in part, improvements to engine noise insulation are so effective. Whine from the turbocharger is barely perceptible, as are induction and exhaust noise."

A few months later, the same magazine carried a full road test.

The early home market models were offered with a strange two-tone paint scheme, the finish lines making the car look very awkward. All Turbos had the option of two-tone coachwork from the 1980 model year, although with a more elegant break separating the lower and upper body. Some combinations were nice, but some were hideous.

A pre-production, American specification Turbo, similar to the car Road & Track tested in Germany in the June 1979 issue. Note the different bumpers and side markers required for the US market.

"Porsche have once again succeeded in cutting down lag (the lapse in performance while the supercharger turbine accelerates back to its working speed – up to 100,000rpm in this case – after the throttle has momentarily shut for any reason) to the one second maximum expected from any good installation," it said.

However, the testers did find the engine "noticeably rough" at times and were less than enamoured by the noises it made – not that it was a particularly noisy unit, but lacking that high-performance exhaust note one expects to hear from a Porsche. Wind noise was also a problem pointed out in several publications.

Handling was generally highly praised by all who tried the car, while the transaxle was able to deal with the additional power with ease. Due to the substantial increase in torque and beefier driveline, the extra work may have caused problems for the synchromesh. However, as *Autocar*

Having subjected the normally-aspirated 924 to the toughest of endurance runs, Austrian enthusiasts, Rudi Lins and Gerhard Plattner, completed a 23,000 mile expedition with the first Turbo off the line. This was perhaps the ultimate test, during which the pair returned an astonishing fuel consumption figure of 22.8mpg.

noted: "We had wondered if this might show up in rougher or slower downchanges. It didn't." Enough said. In addition, "it has superb traction," observed the *Autocar* in a later article. All in all, the transaxle had proved itself more than capable of coping with more horses under the bonnet.

John Bolster was full of praise for the new model: "The Porsche 924 Turbo is a two-litre car that can outperform most of the so-called supercars at a fraction of their bills. It is also sufficiently light and responsive to out-corner them with ease, while its wide revolution range and flat torque curve render it a most un-tiring companion on a journey."

Concerning fuel consumption, the manufacturer quoted 36.2mpg at a steady 56mph, although individual road tests indicated an average of around 20.5mpg after some admittedly hard driving. In normal use, an owner could reasonably expect between 25 to 30 miles to the gallon. With a bigger 14.5 Imperial gallon (66 litre) fuel tank, this gave the car a very useful range.

As for performance, the *Autocar* recorded a top speed of 144mph, with 0-60 being accomplished in just 6.9 seconds. It said: "It is a remarkable machine, quicker than a manual 928, and nearly as quick as the three-litre 911SC."

Writing for *Car & Driver*, Rich Ceppos said "The well-muscled engine, combined with the 924's good brakes and stable, slightly understeering handling, made our foray through the Stuttgart countryside both exciting and memorable. Out on the autobahn,

the 924 Turbo was equally spicy. Set it loose and the scenery blurs, pronto ... The 924 is finally a truly balanced high-performance car, and no excuses or apologies have to be made to anyone, anywhere."

Dr Fuhrmann chose to describe it as "a modest improvement," however, judging by the many rave reviews from around the world, it was anything but modest – it was a transformation. That great enthusiast, Paul Frere, noted: "I think the new Porsche 924 Turbo will go a long way toward getting the breed accepted as a real Porsche among the traditional diehards."

Other 1979 MY news

The Porsche-designed, Getrag five-speed gearbox became standard in the US for the 1979 model year normally-aspirated cars, but the competition, especially from Japan, had also moved up a gear. The 924's $14,600 starting price meant it was far too expensive to worry Datsun and Mazda salesmen. Even the high performance Pontiac Trans-Am, Chevrolet Camaro Z28 and Corvette L82 (which could out-drag the 924 Turbo over the standing-quarter) were cheaper.

The three-speed automatic was still offered, however, and *Road & Track* compared a car equipped with this transmission with its main rivals from the Datsun, Mazda and Chevrolet camps – the all-new 280ZX, RX-7 and Corvette.

The car was already the most expensive in the group, but options such as air conditioning (then $695), a sunroof ($395), leather seat facings

($680), metallic paint ($395) and electric windows ($300) isolated it even further. In view of its excessive price, the R&T testers were quite hard on the Stuttgart machine, stating: "Good fuel economy, striking looks, a fine finish and the best handling in its field are pluses to be envied. But the question is, can they offset the 924's anemic performance, mind-numbing noisiness and high price?" In their opinion, obviously not, as the car finished third, trailing some way behind the two Japanese models.

As tests on the automatic version are quite rare, it is interesting to note what was said regarding the gearbox: "There's no low-end power, a problem compounded by a rather sluggish automatic transmission. Downshifts are not instantaneous (the gearbox pauses before engaging), and this really becomes annoying when one attempts to shift while cornering." Oh dear!

British prices officially started at £8549 for a standard 924, but a more realistic example is the five-speed Lux at £9389 (a four-speed manual or three-speed automatic gearbox were still available for the UK, incidentally). For comparison, at this time, the 911SC was £14,549 (the same as a Lotus Eclat 523), but its more direct competition was still substantially cheaper.

The 924 Turbo was followed a year later by a substantially more powerful Carrera GT model. This lightweight, 210bhp beast was first shown at the 1979 Frankfurt Show, and revealed Porsche's obvious plans to enter the 924 in the field of competition. This important derivative, along with the

93

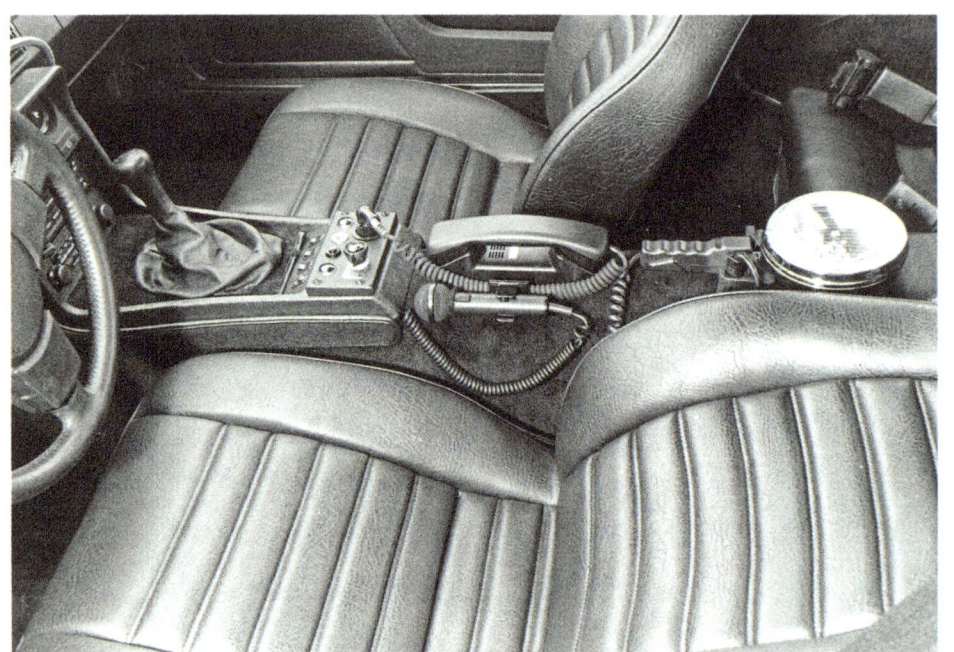

As it had on the normally-aspirated 924, Porsche built a Notarzt fast response vehicle based on the 924 Turbo.

other cars developed from it, will be covered in the next chapter.

On the subject of unusual 924s, the factory continued to build limited edition models. The fully-loaded 'Sebring 79' was produced to celebrate Porsche's racing victories, but was for the US market only. Given the M429 designation and finished in Guards Red with some rather loud badging, a total of 1400 were constructed during the early part of 1979. The 'Cork' model, which aped the earlier Swiss special, was produced shortly after (limited to 300 units), followed by a 100-off, all-black version for Italy; in addition, the UK marketed 50 gold 924s with the Doubloon appellation.

Interior of the Notarzt 924 Turbo. Note the standard three-spoke wheel employed on the turbocharged cars.

The Turbo in the States

The Turbo was officially introduced to the USA in October 1979 as a 1980 model, but a limited run of 600 were sent over in July, doubtless to keep dealers and the press happy. This explains why a number of the early tests carried out in America featured the car with the petrol cap showing: as a 1980 model, this should have been hidden behind a flap.

The engine retained the 7.5:1 compression ratio, but it had a three-way catalytic converter (newly-adopted oxygen sensors ensured it worked efficiently), and a smaller turbocharger than that found on its European counterparts, the two naturally combining to significantly reduce power output. Although people had been expecting 150bhp, the proper figures were actually 143bhp at 5500rpm and 147lbft of torque at 3000rpm, but it was legal in all 50 States.

The United States was also expecting an upgraded chassis to be offered, but, in fact, the original disc/drum braking system could handle the added power more than satisfactorily. Surprisingly, given the vehicle's performance potential, in view of this, to cut costs, Porsche decided this would suffice as the standard specification, although it then had to produce 6J x 15 Turbo-style wheels with a four-bolt fixing.

Rightly, at least Porsche offered the Turbo with the stiffer suspension set-up and disc brakes all-round, albeit as an option – the M471 Sport Group Package. The chassis modifications

American advertising for the 1980 model year, when the Turbo was officially launched in this important market. From 1980, all Turbos came with mudguards fitted to the rear wheelarches.

were also made available on 100 of the normally-aspirated cars (which just so happened to be perfect for SCCA D-Production racing).

In addition, the gearing was adjusted to better suit American road conditions, so the final-drive ratio was altered to 4.71:1 (the same as a non-turbocharged European model) and the fifth gear was changed from 0.71 to 0.60:1. Oddly, the steering was given a different ratio to keep it at four turns lock-to-lock for the US market, prompting some enthusiast

95

Although the Turbo wasn't officially available in the States until the 1980 model year, a number were shipped across in the summer. This is one of the early batch of 924 Turbos sent there in July, showing the car's badging, the new style of two-tone paint scheme, and the four-bolt wheels made for the US market.

publications to say it was a little "slow" for this type of vehicle, and only a front anti-roll bar (21mm in diameter) came as standard.

Inside, the speedometer was marked up to 160mph (later changed to 85mph to comply with new Federal legislation), and the 8000rpm tacho skewed over as on European models. However, items like electric windows and mirrors remained firmly on the option list in a further bid to keep the POE price down.

With less power, different gearing and substantially more weight (the American specification model tipped the scales at 2780lbs, or 1264kg), naturally enough performance was blunted somewhat, compared to the cars for the home market. That said, the 924 Turbo certainly wasn't a slouch.

According to *Road & Track*'s 1000th road test, the top speed was around 131mph – I know that's fairly

academic in a country where the speed limit is so low, but it's always nice to know the potential is there, and overtaking becomes a much safer operation; the standing-quarter could be dismissed in 16.3 seconds at a terminal speed of 88mph, and 0-60 came up in just 7.7 seconds. However, most tests carried out in America showed a great disparity in times.

The US press launch was held in Irvington, Virginia, at the same time as that for the Audi 4000 – the two marques still being linked via Volkswagen in marketing terms in America. *Road & Track* thought it was "super, with the sort of performance the car should have had from the beginning. At last, the acceleration is an appropriate match for the very good handling characteristics.

"The US Turbo is equipped with a three-way catalyst and in temperatures ranging from 10 degrees below freezing

to around 50 degrees Fahrenheit, the engine fired right up with just a few kicks from the starter. And whether hot, cold or somewhere in between, it exhibited excellent warm-up and driveability characteristics."

They loved the new M31 powerplant, which they felt was "tractable and free-revving" and continued: "Boost starts to build at a low 1600rpm and maximum boost of 7 psi is achieved at 2800 revs for the smaller but quicker-revving turbo used on the US engine. (Comparable figures for the European Turbo are 1800rpm and 10psi boost at 2800rpm.)

"The subtlety of the 924 Turbo is quite a contrast to the 930 Carrera that lets you know it's turbocharged with a neck-snapping bang. The 924 Turbo's forgiving nature was especially appreciated on the snow- and ice-covered roads around Stuttgart. I never feared an 'incident' as I might have with the 930's more peaky boost ... However, mild power oversteer is available to the skilled driver, and the extra power allows the chassis' real potential to be realized."

In a later article, in which the 924S Turbo (the Turbo equipped with the M471 option) was reviewed, the testers said: "Most of the car's negative traits are overlooked when the Turbo is flung down some twisty highway at a rapid clip. That's when the finely-tuned suspension, those sticky P7s, incredible brakes and flexible engine work together to produce the excellent balance one hopes for, but doesn't always encounter, in many expensive GTs."

Car & Driver was also clearly impressed, saying the car produced an "indescribably wonderful noise and sensations such as few four-cylinders have ever given before. The five-speed gearbox and its much-improved linkage march you through the gears like the Marine Band."

If there was a problem, it was the price, and it was a serious problem. *Motor Trend* pointed out: "We are ecstatic to see the 924 Turbo offer such a pleasing blend of performance and sheer driving enjoyment, but the price we find to be as inviting as a cod liver oil milkshake."

With a list price of $19,880 before popular options such as air

The US specification 924 Turbo in all its glory.

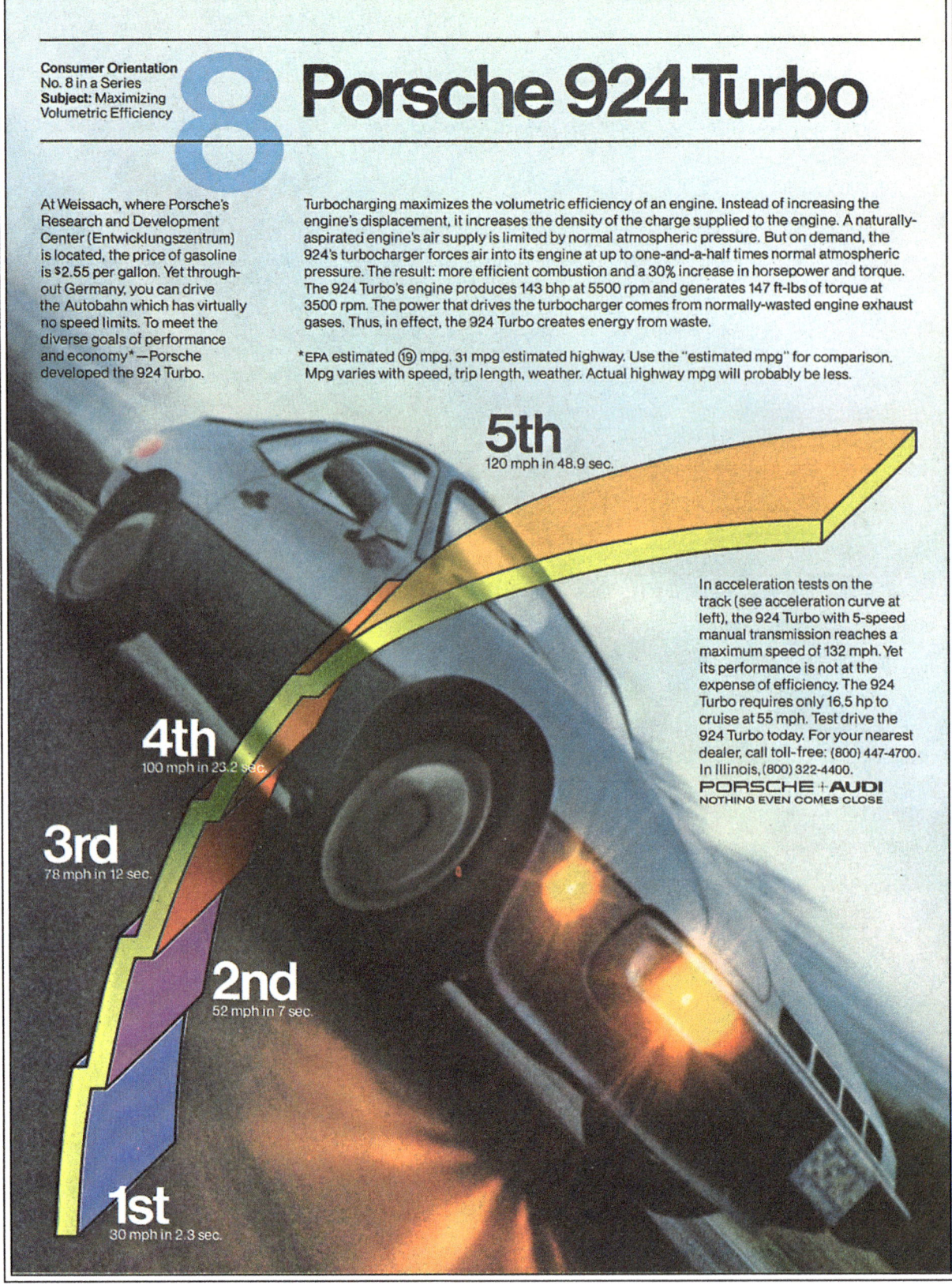

Consumer Orientation
No. 8 in a Series
Subject: Maximizing
Volumetric Efficiency

8

Porsche 924 Turbo

At Weissach, where Porsche's Research and Development Center (Entwicklungszentrum) is located, the price of gasoline is $2.55 per gallon. Yet throughout Germany, you can drive the Autobahn which has virtually no speed limits. To meet the diverse goals of performance and economy*—Porsche developed the 924 Turbo.

Turbocharging maximizes the volumetric efficiency of an engine. Instead of increasing the engine's displacement, it increases the density of the charge supplied to the engine. A naturally-aspirated engine's air supply is limited by normal atmospheric pressure. But on demand, the 924's turbocharger forces air into its engine at up to one-and-a-half times normal atmospheric pressure. The result: more efficient combustion and a 30% increase in horsepower and torque. The 924 Turbo's engine produces 143 bhp at 5500 rpm and generates 147 ft-lbs of torque at 3500 rpm. The power that drives the turbocharger comes from normally-wasted engine exhaust gases. Thus, in effect, the 924 Turbo creates energy from waste.

*EPA estimated ⑲ mpg. 31 mpg estimated highway. Use the "estimated mpg" for comparison. Mpg varies with speed, trip length, weather. Actual highway mpg will probably be less.

5th
120 mph in 48.9 sec.

4th
100 mph in 23.2 sec.

3rd
78 mph in 12 sec.

2nd
52 mph in 7 sec.

1st
30 mph in 2.3 sec.

In acceleration tests on the track (see acceleration curve at left), the 924 Turbo with 5-speed manual transmission reaches a maximum speed of 132 mph. Yet its performance is not at the expense of efficiency. The 924 Turbo requires only 16.5 hp to cruise at 55 mph. Test drive the 924 Turbo today. For your nearest dealer, call toll-free: (800) 447-4700. In Illinois, (800) 322-4400.

PORSCHE + AUDI
NOTHING EVEN COMES CLOSE

A 924 Turbo for the British market.

Interior of the same car with the Pasha interior seat trim. Note the new tachometer, rotated fractionally anti-clockwise to make it easier to read through the steering wheel (the red line was at 6600rpm, at which point the rev limiter cut in); UK specification speedometers read to 160mph, while the German Turbo had a 260kph clock. Gauge markings were in green initially on the Turbos, but later changed to white on black, and there was 'Turbo' script on the door sills.

conditioning (an extra $750), a sunroof ($440), dual electrically-adjusted mirrors ($190), headlight washers ($170), rear wiper ($235), a limited-slip differential ($590), sports shock absorbers ($145), a rear anti-roll bar ($85), electric windows ($300) and stereo equipment were added, this was by no means a poor man's Porsche. And two-tone paintwork was very expensive at the best part of $900.

As an enthusiast, if one went for the Sport Group Package, including ventilated disc brakes all-round, 205/55 VR16 Pirelli P7 tyres on 6J disc-type forged alloy rims (with a five-bolt fixing to suit the new hubs), the uprated shock absorbers, a 23mm front and 14mm rear anti-roll bar, the smaller leather-trimmed four-spoke steering wheel and an 'S' decal, there wouldn't be much change out of $2000.

In reality, the fact that the disc brakes didn't come as standard was a bit naughty and incensed many, but somehow, in the face of a strong German currency and weakening dollar, Porsche just had to keep the price below that magic $20,000 mark.

It was a great shame that this had to be done, as it took some of the gloss off the model. However, we will leave the final words to *Car & Driver*, which

Porsche Cars Great Britain Limited, Richfield Avenue, Reading RG1 8PH. Telephone: 0734 595411.
For Tourist, NATO, Diplomatic and Personal Export enquires Tel: 01-568 1313. The present Porsche line up consists of ten models: the four cylinder
924 Series from £9,104; the six cylinder 911 Series from £16,109 and the eight cylinder 928 Series from £21,827. Prices, correct at time of going
to press, exclude number plates and delivery. For further information and details of leasing facilities contact your nearest official Porsche Centre.

erman Mustard.

The most powerful two litre production car in the world. The Porsche 924 Turbo.

Nothing compares.

Autocar tried, in their Autotest.* But found it necessary to choose more expensive cars as their bench-mark.

They didn't do too well.

At 142 m.p.h. the 924 Turbo was faster than the Porsche 911 SC, BMW 635 CSi and Lotus Eclat 523.

0-60 m.p.h. in 6.9 seconds made it quicker than an Aston Martin V8, the Lotus or BMW.

Returning 19.8 m.p.g. it proved to be more economical than the Porsche 911 SC, BMW and Aston Martin.

Only once did we come way behind.

In price.

£13,630.

PORSCHE **924** *turbo*

Early British advertising for the 924 Turbo, which made its debut at £13,629. At that time, the 911 range started at £16,109, with the 928 priced from £21,827.

concluded: "The Porsche 924 Turbo may be a far cry from the cars that looked like bathtubs and sounded like Beetles, but in philosophy it's not really all that different from its predecessors: fast, expensive, and exclusive. Proof, you might say, that the more Porsches change, the more they stay the same."

The Turbo reaches the UK

Early reports had the 924 Turbo earmarked for introduction to the UK market in autumn 1979, and it made its official debut at the Earls Court Show in October. All cars sold in Britain had the 928-style, four-spoke steering wheel, electric windows with tinted glass, an electrically-adjusted and heated driver's door mirror, headlight washers, a rear wiper and a Panasonic stereo radio/cassette as standard.

Cars for the European mainland were equipped with a Spacesaver spare (an electric air pump and dial-type pressure gauge were included in the comprehensive tool kit to enable it to be pumped up). However, these were outlawed in the UK, so a full-size spare wheel and tyre was supplied for the British market.

In a full *Motor Sport* test, Clive Richardson was a little more impressed than after his brief acquaintance with the new model in Germany. He said: "How wrong I was! After some 900 miles with the road test car, I was almost as loath to hand it back to Porsche as I am with 911s. The 924 Turbo is not perfect, but is supremely fast, extraordinarily economical in relation to performance, practical, comfortable and at times very exciting."

A left-hand drive Turbo for the European mainland. Turbocharged cars were still quite a rarity at this time, although this form of forced induction had been introduced to the F1 scene by Renault in 1977, bringing it to the attention of a much wider audience.

Motor magazine described it as "a supercar of the future." The report noted: "The spoilers fitted to the Turbo ensure that it runs arrow-straight even when close to its [140mph] maximum speed. This, together with wind noise that, while noticeable at 70mph, doesn't become much worse at higher speeds, makes cruising at very high speeds relaxed. With a long-legged gait of 24.4mph per 1000rpm, even 120mph represents only 4900rpm in fifth. Mechanical trash is low, too."

John Bolster, *Autosport*'s long-serving anchor man, also felt the new car was much quieter, stating that "the tyre roar that used to be so prominent in the 924 has virtually been eliminated, though some bump-thump is still noticeable ... The turbocharger is seldom audible and though the engine is not silent, it is smoother than that of the normal 924." He added: "One sits fairly low in the car but the all-round view is quite satisfactory, except for the shortest drivers ... The small

steering wheel and gearlever are well placed and instrument dials are easy to read, though, regrettably, there is no boost gauge."

He thought the gearchange itself was a little awkward, and the clutch a touch on the heavy side, but was very enthusiastic about the vehicle's handling: "The car has a 50-50 weight distribution, and a high polar moment of inertia, due to the separation of the engine and transmission. Certainly, the results are very impressive

indeed, the cornering power being extraordinary, while the stability at maximum speed is first class. The steering is not particularly quick, but the rear end does not break away, the handling being virtually neutral under all conditions." However, in a later report, Bolster pointed out that "this exemplary behaviour is not repeated on wet and slippery surfaces."

The *Autocar* said the driving environment was "comfortable and sensible" and reported that the "ride is firm. You get jarred noticeably but not unacceptably over sharp bumps. The car doesn't seem, however, to be disturbed seriously if it hits a bump in a bend. It does roll, but not much, so that combined with the handling and grip, it's a car which invites fast driving at any time."

A moody shot used in the 1980 model year catalogue.

The 924 Turbo – pride of Germany.

It concluded: "Naturally, this Turbo has the usual shortcomings of such a car, but they are a small and insignificant price to pay for almost infinitely safer handling than the 911's. It is a wonderful machine which is a tonic to drive. The three-litre SC will always have its devotees, and deservedly so – no turbo four can compare for the excitement of that superb flat-six – but it comes very close, and is assuredly much easier to drive."

Running on four-star fuel, the *Autocar* managed an average of 19.8mpg during its test, managing over 25 in gentler moments. Given its performance – which was basically on a par with that of the much more expensive Ferrari 308 GT4, Aston Martin V8 and the fabulous Maserati Merak supercars – economy was also excellent.

Motor made an interesting comment: "All of our testers were impressed by the 924 Turbo's finish. Unlike early 924s, it looks much more of a car in the traditional Porsche mould, with immaculate paint finish, superbly fitted doors, and an interior colour blend that's both soothing and tasteful. With the Lux specification as standard, the Turbo is also as well equipped as any rival."

Although it still had a few familiar niggling faults (such as the low-set steering wheel), which car didn't during this period? As a package, it had few rivals at its price (the Turbo was initially listed at £13,629 – £4047 more than a standard five-speed 924 Lux), making it a very different proposition to its normally-aspirated stablemate.

Other 1980 model year news

As well as being fitted on the Turbo, all US 1980 model year cars (including the 911 and 928) came equipped with an oxygen sensor. The Lambda-sond sensor screwed into the exhaust manifold and, in conjunction with the fuel-injection system, constantly varied the air-fuel mix to give the most efficient burn, thus allowing the newly-adopted, three-way catalytic converter to do its job of cutting down CO, HC and NOx emissions; it also enhanced engine response and fuel consumption, the latter by as much as 20%.

This enabled Porsche to raise the compression ratio to 9.0:1, and

qualified the engine (which carried the VC designation) as suitable for sale in all 50 States and Japan. Driveability was improved, as was power output, now quoted as being 115bhp at 5750rpm; peak torque was still 111lbft at 3500rpm.

A new Audi five-speed transmission was introduced with fifth up and to the right and reverse below like the contemporary Alfas. This arrangement received a more favourable reception from most, although I must say I've always rather liked the dog-leg first layout. Anyway, the availability of this cheaper five-speed unit made it viable for use as the standard transmission in all markets for the normally-aspirated 924, augmented by the old three-speed automatic. (The Turbo retained the Getrag Type G31 'box, as the Audi unit wasn't able to handle the additional torque.)

In the States, the ratios were 3.60:1 on first, 2.13 on second, 1.36 on third, 0.97 on fourth, and 0.73:1 on top, while the final-drive ratio

The European market Porsche line-up for 1980. It includes (clockwise from the right): the 924, 924 Turbo, 911SC, 911 Turbo, 911SC Targa, 928 and the new 4.7 litre 928S.

was 4.11:1 (the latter was 3.89:1 in Europe). Performance figures for the US specification model revealed a 0-60 time of 10.6 seconds, with the standing-quarter being dismissed in 17.6 at a terminal speed of 78mph.

The ride was further enhanced, *Road & Track* noting: "It's firm as always, but much of the terrible harshness and vibration of earlier versions has been isolated and/or damped to a livable level. It's certainly not perfect, but it is sufficiently better to rate with the best in its class."

For 1980 proper, side window frames were all black, and the fuel filler was concealed behind a plastic flap to give the off-side flank a cleaner look; naturally, these were a feature on both the turbocharged and normally-aspirated 924s. (With the catalyst, only unleaded petrol could be used, although European models were still running on four-star leaded fuel, incidentally.)

There was a new, larger brake servo (the same as that used on the Turbo), a wider range of trim options, and the improved sound-proofing found on the Turbo was carried over to the lower-powered model, prompting *Road & Track* to call the latest version

"a much more refined and quiet car."

The German magazine, *Auto Motor und Sport*, again voted the 924 the 'Best Sports Car' in the under two-litre class for 1980, making it four times in a row that the baby Porsche had taken the title. Unfortunately, the cost of 924 motoring was still climbing. With a list price of $15,970 (which soon shot up to $16,770), it cost almost twice as much as a Mazda RX-7 GS (listed at $8295) and around $6000 more than a Datsun 280ZX: to add insult to injury, both of these were faster, quieter and better-equipped.

Adding options such as the

Standard coachwork colours (1980 MY)

Mocha Black, Lilac, Mexico Beige, Guards Red, Malaga Red, Monaco Blue, Amethyst, Venus Red, Alpine White.

Special coachwork colours

Petrol Blue Metallic, Onyx Metallic, Minerva Blue Metallic, Indiana Red Metallic, Dolomite Grey Metallic, Diamond Silver Metallic.

Dual tone colours

Mexico Beige over Mocha Black, Alpine White over Mexico Beige, Alpine White over Guards Red, Inari Silver Metallic over Onyx Metallic, Diamond Silver Metallic over Helios Blue Metallic, Diamond Silver Metallic over Dolomite Grey Metallic.

Trim materials

Black, Brown or Beige leatherette with matching inlays. Alternatively, inlays could be in Tartan Dress cloth (Green/Black, Red/Black or Grey/Blue/Black), a chequered Pasha velour (Grey/Black or Beige/Brown), or Pinstripe velour (Black with White or Brown with Beige); seat facings could also be supplied in Black, Brown or Beige leather as an option. Carpets came in Black, Brown or Beige.

1979 model year 924 photographs of this car were later retouched for the 1980 catalogue, as the fuel filler cap was placed behind a cover for that season, although the car does carry 1980-style seat trim. Note the new badges, changed to decals for the 1979 MY to fit in with the Turbo.

Interior of the same car, with its tasteful pinstripe velour seat inlays.

$1620 E82 package (including air conditioning, sunroof, electrically-adjustable heated door mirrors and the smaller, four-spoke leather-trimmed steering wheel), or the $1575 Handling Package (disc brakes all-round, Turbo-specification anti-roll bars, sports shock absorbers, cast alloy wheels with Pirelli P6 tyres, and a leather steering wheel), not to mention stereo equipment (between $200 and $700), meant it moved even further away from its supposed competition.

In England, after comparing a Datsun 280ZX 2+2 automatic, a Ford Capri 3000 Ghia, a Reliant Scimitar GTE and a Vauxhall Royale coupé with the 924 Lux, the *Autocar* noted in its issue of 13 October 1979: "If it is performance and handling [that are your priorities], the 924 wins easily, with its excellent road manners and a complete (if slightly antiseptic) lack of the handling temperament of its famous rear-engined brothers."

Incidentally, the age of the four-wheel drive rally car came with the launch of the Audi Quattro

in March 1980. Ferdinand Piech, Audi's Technical Director at the time, approved the project, with the first prototype being ready in late-1977. Its World Rally Championship debut came on the 1981 Monte Carlo Rally, and from 1982 to 1984, Audi dominated the rallying scene. It is interesting to note that Ferry Porsche had suggested a 4wd Passat to Volkswagen as early as 1974, but for one reason or another the project failed to get off the ground.

Meanwhile, the 924 was establishing a competition record, discussed in the next chapter. Following the 1980 Le Mans, Porsche produced a limited edition version of the 924 by that name. Finished in white with a black interior and unique side stripes, it came with 6J x 15 Turbo-style, multi-spoke alloys (but with a four-stud fitting instead of five), 205/60 HR15 tyres, and a rear spoiler borrowed from the turbocharged car to give it added exclusivity. Just 100 were allocated to the UK market – around 10% of the 1030 production run.

British advertising for the 1980 model year 924, with prices starting at £9104. For 1980, an automatic gearbox (normally-aspirated cars only) would have cost £478; electric door mirrors now came as standard in the UK.

noney we designed a car
ver £9,000.

cceleration to match, the 924 returns
tions. And, when driven at a constant
e Fiat Strada 65CL.)
every 12,000 miles or annually.
than those of a Mini.*
he price suggests, spare no expense

sten all components by hand.
nd five speed gear pattern as in the

vith front mounted engine and
Porsche 928.
galvanised steel sheeting and give a

24 keeps its value come resale.
our money's worth.

Left, main picture: A 1980 German-registered 924. All cars from the start of the 1980 model year had a full black finish on the side window frames.

Inset, left: The normally-aspirated 'Le Mans' limited edition model of 1980. That year, the 924 made its debut at the famous Sarthe track.

Inset, right: Interior of the 924 'Le Mans' special, complete with the slightly smaller four-spoke steering wheel.

Tailpiece.

PORSCHE 924

5

THE 924 IN COMPETITION

Tony Dron, winner of the 1978 924 Challenge Trophy.

Jurgen Barth gave the 924 its rallying debut, and later drove for the works at Le Mans.

A February 1978 issue of *Autocar* announced that a 924 Challenge Trophy racing series had just been instigated in the UK. The brainchild of John Aldington, Managing Director of Porsche Cars GB Ltd, and Mike Cotton (the same concern's PR man), this one-make championship ran for one year, with top saloon and sports car drivers campaigning 12 similar 924s around the race tracks of Britain.

The title eventually went to Tony Dron, who had won six rounds. Tony's Broadspeed-prepared car had been entered by Gordon Ramsay, a Newcastle-based Porsche dealer. Multiple BTCC Champion Andy Rouse won the other three rounds to take second place, recording the greatest number of fastest laps along the way. Both would feature later on in the 924s competition history.

The winning 924 had a brief history after this in the hands of Geoff Fox and Richard Bond, but then fell into a state of neglect. The five-speed car resurfaced again in 1988, and later appeared in restored condition in a *Classic Cars* article conducted by none other than Tony Dron – then Editor of the magazine.

The 924 in rallying

Jurgen Barth, a Porsche stalwart, was due to give the 924 Turbo its WRC debut on the 1979 Monte Carlo Rally, although a delay in getting the homologation papers through meant the pre-production Turbo model had to be converted back to a normally-aspirated car.

Starting from Frankfurt (one of nine starting points that entrants could chose from that year), and with Roland Kussmaul (Porsche's Chief Test Driver) as co-driver, Barth took car number 40 (LB-ZL 366) to 20th overall by the time the event came to an end on 26 January.

After the 924 Turbo was eventually homologated in February (homologation no. 660), Barth took a two-car team to the 1979 Safari Rally. The turbocharged cars produced 170bhp in Group 4 trim, a useful 45bhp gain over the normally-aspirated

The SCCA racers had the M471 suspension and braking package but with aluminium shock absorbers, titanium alloy coil-springs, BBS alloy wheels and a number of lightweight body modifications.

model, although the additional weight brought about by the turbo installation and the strengthening necessary for such a harsh event negated much of the advantage.

The Safari Rally ran from 12 to 16 April, mostly in dry conditions. Again, sponsorship came from the Datacom concern, but, sadly, both cars failed to finish the gruelling 3000 mile event; in fact, out of 66 cars to start the 1979 Safari, only 21 made it to Nairobi. The Barth/Kussmaul vehicle (number 20, registration LB-ZL 366), after numerous difficulties, finally succumbed to transmission trouble on the last day, while number 26, the Alex

Engines were tuned to give around 175bhp, though it was found that substituting the normally-aspirated cylinder head with the one from the Turbo released a few extra horses. Dry sump lubrication was employed, and a slight increase in the bore took the displacement to 2039cc.

Janda car, suffered from fuel-injection problems caused by dust penetration. As a matter of interest, a Datsun 160J won the rally, with that other mighty Stuttgart manufacturer, Mercedes-Benz, coming in second ahead of a Fiat.

Jurgen Barth returned to Monte

Interior of an SCCA racer prepared at Weissach.

The SCCA races had provided Datsun and the British Leyland organisation with a lot of good publicity. Now Porsche wanted a piece of the action, and duly won the D-Production title in 1980 and 1981.

Carlo in 1980. Starting from Frankfurt (number 27) in a 924 Turbo, he finished the event 19th overall.

SCCA racing

In the States, the Sports Car Club of America (SCCA) races have always been important from a publicity point of view. The 924 didn't feature in the results of the SCCA Run-Offs in 1979 (or the years running up to it – nor did its main rival, the RX-7, for that matter), although it should be noted that the Scirocco had been competing successfully for quite some time.

Road & Track carried this snippet in its February 1979 issue: "Almost as interesting as Porsche's IMSA plans are the firm's SCCA strategies. Although the factory has participated in the club's professional series, the

Trans-Am, they have expressed little or no interest in amateur racing in the production car classes. Until this year. For 1979, Porsche is readying the improved 924 for D-Production. At this time, Al Holbert and Peter Gregg are slated to receive cars (Holbert says he'll put racing co-ordinator, Doc Bundy, in his car, while Gregg intimates he'd consider 'someone like Robert Overby,' the current SCCA E-Production champion). But word is that the factory would like to fill the field with 924s, so it wouldn't surprise me if other teams also received cars."

In all, 16 modified and M471-equipped 924s were built in Stuttgart, then shipped to the States to compete in the D-Production category. The car made its competition debut at the 1979 Run-Offs, where Al Holbert and Joe

114

Doc Bundy after winning the 1980 SCCA D-Production title.

Below: Ken Williams literally taking the flag in the Road Atlanta SCCA Run-Offs, October 1980.

One of the three prototypes built for the 1979 Frankfurt Show. Note the bulging wing lines, Fuchs wheels borrowed from the 911, slightly larger rear spoiler and air intake on the bonnet.

Herman both entered cars, inviting Tom Robertson and Tom Brennan to drive for them, as Holbert and Herman hadn't got enough points to qualify for the finals themselves. They didn't win, but Porsche sent a clear message to the Datsun and BL camps.

1980 was the key year. After almost being disqualified, Ken Williams won the Showroom Stock A title, while the all-important D-Production honours went to Doc Bundy. Bundy's 924 beat the Triumphs of Wilson and Mueller, and later he made an appearance at Le Mans with the model.

In 1981, Ken Williams could only manage a second place in the SS/A category, beaten by a Ford Mustang Turbo, but Porsche dominated the D-Production race. Although shortened because of poor weather, there was no doubt Tom Brennan deserved his win in the 924, and was followed home by Bundy in a similar model. Third place went to Donald Istook in a 911T.

The 1982 D-Production title was hard-fought. Lotus driver David Vegher narrowly beat former E-Production Champion, and now 924 campaigner, John O'Steen. Bob Hagestad was third in another 924, being chased by a gaggle of British machinery. Vegher

retained his title in the following year, again at the expense of 924 drivers, this time John Schneider and Steven Pieper.

Tom Brennan won the 1985 GT-3

category with his 924, but already the model was starting to feature in results less and less. In reality, the cars sent from Germany had already done their job, raising the profile of the breed

This prototype bears a striking resemblance to the forthcoming 944.

The third car prepared for the 1979 Frankfurt Show. The rear wheelarch extensions are slightly different, and cover the optional 6J x 16 forged alloy wheels offered for the Turbo (fitted with 225/50-section VR-rated rubber in this case).

at a crucial time in its development. Meanwhile, in Europe, there was a lot of press excitement.

The Carrera GT

The 924 Carrera GT model was first shown at the 1979 Frankfurt Show as a "styling exercise," but revealed Porsche's obvious intent to enter the 924 in competition. Three different Turbo-based prototypes were built, eventually providing the basis for the GT and the forthcoming 944.

Meanwhile, sure enough, in the early part of 1980 a racing model did appear, and was duly given the legendary Carrera appellation. The

glassfibre wing extensions covered enormous Dunlop tyres mounted on 16-inch BBS alloys, and the same lightweight material was also employed for the deep front airdam, bonnet and doors. The side and rear windows were made in plexiglass in a bid to further reduce weight.

Although capacity was kept to 1984cc, the power unit featured a 6.8:1 compression ratio, titanium conrods, a larger turbocharger, air-to-air intercooler, Kugelfischer fuel-injection system and dry sump lubrication. With this specification, it developed a reliable 320bhp at 7000rpm and 282lbft of torque at 4500rpm.

These new cars, weighing in at 2068lbs (940kg), were based on the SCCA racers, so had a coil-spring rear suspension, while the braking system (complete with adjustable brake balance) was borrowed from the 917. In keeping with its objective – to win at Le Mans – it was given a 26.4 gallon (120 litre) fuel tank. Despite the massive wheelarch bulges, the Cd was quoted as being just 0.35.

Testing took place at the Paul Ricard track in France, with Derek Bell and Jacky Ickx behind the wheel. A 30-hour endurance session at the same circuit in April saw Bell, Andy Rouse, Tony Dron and works tester, Gunther

One of the three cars built for the 1980 Le Mans 24-hour classic. Testing at the Paul Ricard circuit revealed one or two problems, but, for a new design, it was remarkably reliable.

Steckkonig, doing the driving. An isolated transmission problem didn't manifest itself in the race, but sadly a burnt exhaust valve did.

Porsche eventually homologated the 1984cc 924 Carrera GT as a Group 4/Group B machine (homologation number 672). However, to qualify, at least 400 examples were needed. Consequently, road cars found their way onto the market, but more on those later.

1980 Le Mans

The Porsche 936 hadn't won the 24-hour classic since 1977, but, despite the fact the ageing sports racers were favourites for victory this year, Dr Fuhrmann decided to leave the works cars in Stuttgart in order to concentrate the team's efforts on the 924.

Fuhrmann had always strived to adopt a policy of having a close relationship between race and road cars, so although some members of the press expressed their surprise, it wasn't really that great a shock. Besides, 935s (variations on the 911) had filled the first three spots in 1979, so there was still a good chance that a Porsche would take the flag.

The factory entered three 924 Carrera GT models in the GTP Class for 1980, signifying the 924's debut at the famous Sarthe track. With highly-modified bodywork hiding 320bhp turbocharged engines, and five-speed Porsche transmissions, the cars were expected to uphold the company's enviable reputation at Le Mans.

Number 2 was driven by BTCC exponents Andy Rouse and Tony

Rear of the same vehicle displaying its massive 16-inch BBS alloy wheels fitted with Dunlop racing tyres. As so few had been built at this stage, the factory was forced to enter it in the GT Prototype (GTP) category, where even Porsche officials expected the car to be out-classed.

Dron; after a brief spark plug change, it came home 12th on distance, still misfiring due to a burnt valve, having covered 2630.7 miles at an average of 109.6mph. Without problems, the pair could have finished much higher, and Dron later described the 924 as "the best-handling car I've ever raced." Derek Bell should have been a third driver in this equipe, but had to replace Peter Gregg in the US team at the last

minute.

Number 3 was duly driven by Bell and Al Holbert, and, having covered 2585.4 miles, was placed 13th overall, sixth in Class. Incidentally, this vehicle featured an American flag on the bonnet to represent the nationality of the drivers (at least it should have been an all-US team), whereas the Rouse/Dron 924 had a British flag.

The third car (number 4) had a

Workman-like interior of the 1980 Le Mans car.

German flag on the bonnet, as this was driven by Jurgen Barth and Manfred Schurti. This was the best-placed 924, coming sixth overall and third in Class after completing 2678.5 miles in the allotted 24 hours. It would have probably done even better but for a damaged radiator, sustained in the night after a run-in with a suicidal rabbit.

Of the 24 Porsches that started at Le Mans in 1980, only ten finished the course that year. However, three of those were the 924 Carrera GT models, which had been running as high as sixth, seventh and ninth three-quarters of the way into the race, thus confirming the 924's position as a worthy example of the Stuttgart marque. The rain-soaked event was won by a Rondeau.

The Carrera GT road car

As mentioned earlier, to homologate the 924 Carrera GT, a minimum of 400 had to be completed. As a result, Porsche decided to offer it as a road car – ultimately, a total of 406 were produced, about half of the run remaining in Germany, while 75 of them were right-hand drive models for the UK. This was not only a rare car, but also highly desirable, and the entire allocation for the British Isles was sold before they were built, despite a £19,210 price tag! None were officially exported to the USA.

Compared to the standard 924 Turbo, it was easy to identify the Carrera. At the front, there was an air intake on the bonnet, and a deeper front spoiler which merged gently into the wider wings, made in reinforced

The beautifully-prepared engine bay.

polyurethane. The rear wheelarches were far bigger, too, with the inner sections larger than standard to allow for racing rubber to be fitted (interestingly, because this model didn't inherit the coil-spring rear suspension of the pure racers, there was a cut-out behind the wheelarch extensions to allow easy access to the torsion bar tube). Around the back, there was a deeper glassfibre bumper, a bigger spoiler and discreet 'Carrera GT' badge. As a result of these bodywork changes, the Cd was just 0.34, and the weight a very reasonable 2594lbs (1179kg).

With a KKK turbocharger, air-to-air intercooler (the latter lurking under the bonnet scoop, and allowing an 8.5:1 compression ratio) and Siemens-

Below: Car number 4 during the ultimate endurance test. It was hoped that the two-litre machine would be able to achieve 185mph down the Mulsanne Straight. Although this wasn't fast by GTP standards, the 924 was remarkably more fuel-efficient, which meant it spent less time in the pits.

Inset: Al Holbert was an important figure in the 924's competition history.

The Rouse/Dron car taking the flag to finish 12th overall.

The Barth/Schurti 924 at speed, on its way to a highly-creditable sixth overall.

Manfred Schurti (seen here) and Jurgen Barth drove the highest-placed 924 at Le Mans in 1980. Norbert Singer was Team Manager for the event.

Fuhrmann was right in that people could relate much easier to racers that looked like road cars. This advert appeared in a number of enthusiast publications across America shortly after Le Mans, and naturally featured the Bell/Holbert machine with its patriotic paintwork.

Engine bay of the Carrera GT, introduced in August 1980.

The purposeful tail of the Type 937, or 924 Carrera GT road car (the 938 number was allocated to right-hand drive versions). The wheelarch extensions and front spoiler were made in reinforced polyurethane, incidentally. It was only available in red, black or silver, whilst interiors were finished in black velour with contrasting pinstripe.

Publicity shot showing the Carrera GT with the Barth/ Schurti Le Mans car and the wonderful pre-war V16 Auto Union.

Another view of the 924 Carrera GT road car. Note the 'Carrera' script, which appeared atop the off-side front wing only, and the flush-fitting windscreen.

Hartig digital ignition (a first for a production car), the two-litre M31/50 engine produced 210bhp at 6000rpm and a healthy 203lbft of torque at 3500rpm. Combined with the Turbo specification, five-speed gearbox – albeit strengthened – and a 3.89:1 final-drive ratio, this was enough to endow the vehicle with a 0-60 time of 6.9 seconds (one independent test recorded an amazing 5.8) and a top speed in excess of 150mph. Not only that, but Porsche claimed it was the most economical car in the range.

The suspension – a subtly uprated version of the Turbo set-up – rode a fraction lower than standard, reducing the car's overall height by about 13mm. Wheels were either Fuchs 7J x 15 forged alloys (equipped with 215/60 Pirelli rubber), or optionally 7J x 16 front and 8J x 16 rear. The last-mentioned items were mounted with 205/55 and 225/50 tyres respectively.

Inside, the car was trimmed in black velour with contrasting pinstripes on the seat facings and door panels. A three-spoke steering wheel from the Turbo was standard, although UK specification models came with the smaller four-spoke item. Power windows and an electrically-adjustable driver's door mirror were also part of the package, with cars destined for British shores having the added benefit of a rear wiper and a Panasonic stereo radio/cassette with electric aerial.

Optional extras, other than those already mentioned, included a limited-slip differential, air conditioning, a sunroof, heated electric passenger door mirror, headlight washers, and a cassette and coin holder. The fuel tank, by the way, had a capacity of 18.5 US gallons, or around 63 litres.

It is interesting to note that the Earl of March, the man behind the revival of the Goodwood racing circuit, named the 924 Carrera GT road car in his top ten favourite automobiles. The Porsche was given the number five slot, ahead of such greats as the Porsche 550, Aston Martin DBR1 and Alfa Romeo P3. The Earl bought his example in 1981, and has kept it as his everyday vehicle ever since.

Mel Nichols, a Motor Trend regular, described it as "perhaps the best road-going Porsche yet." But for those who couldn't afford the real thing, or were too slow placing an order, Dage Sport of Buckinghamshire was quick to offer replica body kits. In 1983, these cost around £745.

The GTS and GTR

The 924 Carrera GTS was built as an Evolution model of the GT. Just 59 were constructed (a minimum of 50 were required by the FIA), with 20% more power and around 124lbs, or 56kg less weight. As a result, the top speed was over 155mph, with the factory quoting a 0-60 time of 6.2 seconds.

The front end and bonnet were made in fibreglass, with a Turbo-style nose panel surrounded by fixed headlights covered in plexiglass; plexiglass was also used for the side and rear windows. The interior was largely stripped out, featuring lightweight bucket seats with racing harnesses and a built-in rollcage.

Despite a lower 8.0:1 compression ratio when compared to the 'normal' GT, due to a 20% increase in the turbo boost, power output was upped to 245bhp at 6250rpm, with a corresponding improvement in peak torque – now 236lbft. To keep the extra horsepower in check, 16-inch wheels and tyres (the ones offered as an option on the GT), and larger 911 Turbo brakes were employed, along with a 40% limited-slip differential.

The 924 Carrera GTR also appeared in 1981, and was a customer racing car built as a result of lessons learnt at Le Mans last year. Weighing just 2112lbs (960kg) in Group 4 trim, the 375bhp engine was enough to give blistering performance and a 180mph top speed. Brakes were sourced from the 917/930, while the standard alloys were 11.5J x 16 items.

All this costs money, approximately £43,000, to be precise; for those with smaller budgets, there was always the 280bhp rally version at a mere £34,000. Nevertheless, 17 GTRs were built in all.

1981 Le Mans

There was the usual varied selection of Porsches at Le Mans in 1981, numbering 18 in all. Of these, three were 924-based machines. Car number 1 was a works-entered 924 GTP driven by Jurgen Barth and 1980 World Rally Champion, Walter Rohrl. Having recorded an average speed of 114mph over the 24 hours, it was eventually placed seventh overall, and third in the GTP Class behind two Rondeaus.

This unique car was powered by a 2479cc version of the four-cylinder engine, the same capacity as the

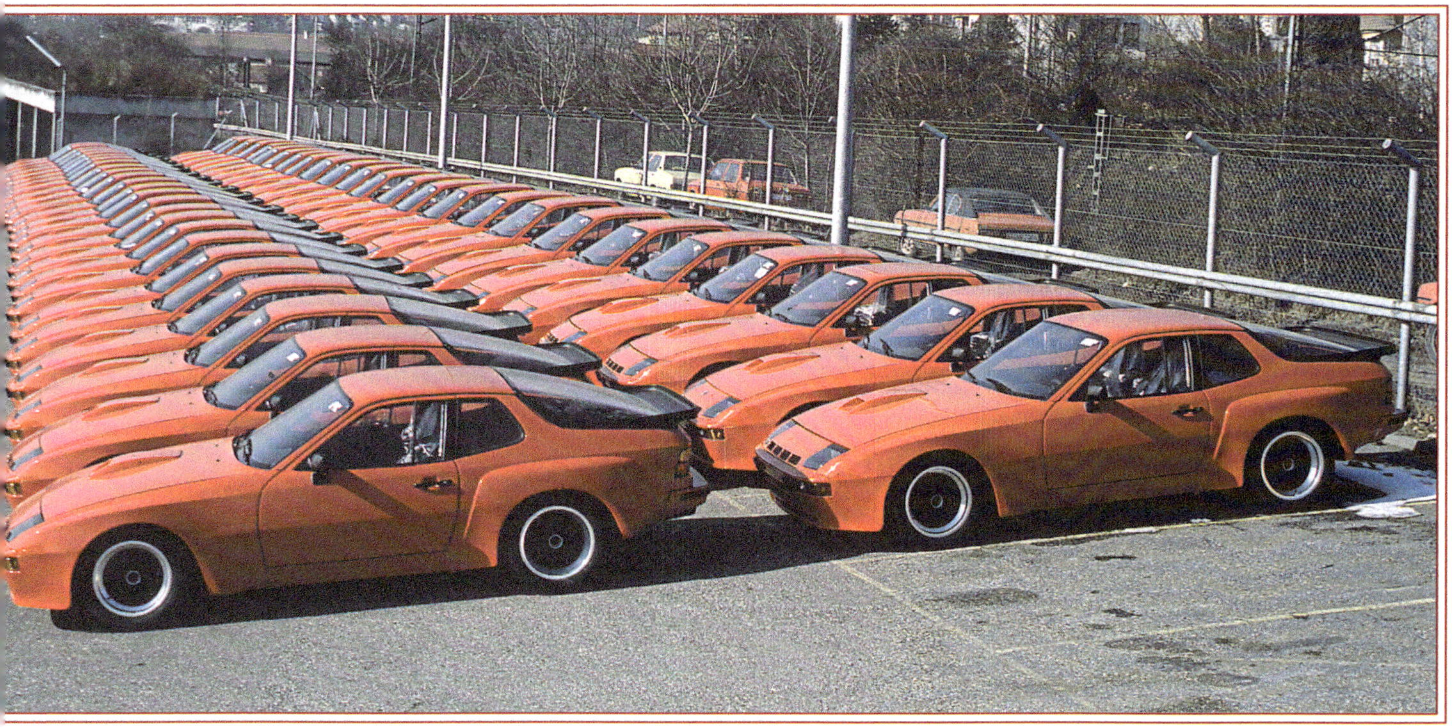

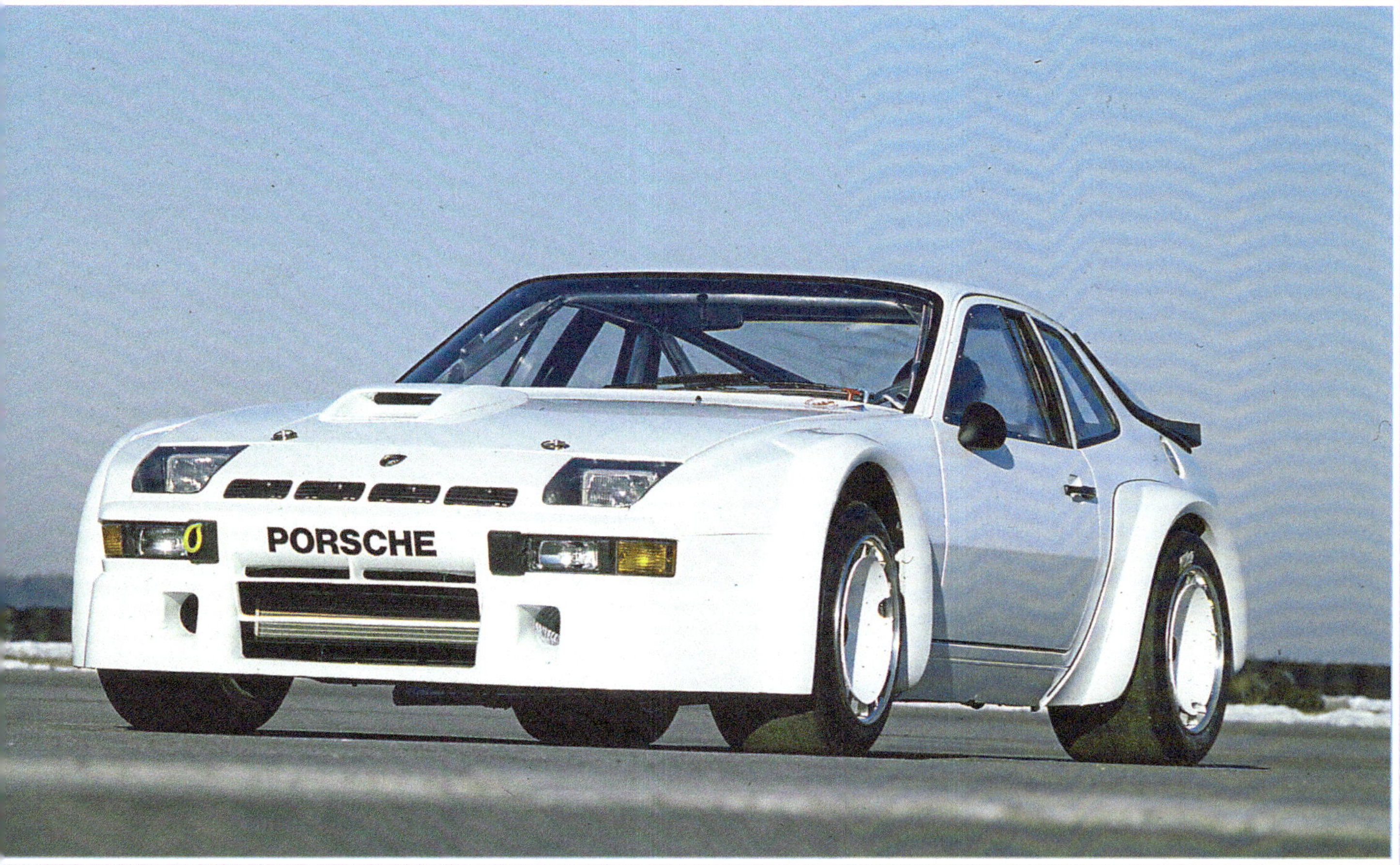
PORSCHE

Final preparation for Le Mans 1981. The car in the foreground is the race-winning 936 of Bell and Ickx.

forthcoming 944 road car. However, with a 16-valve head and KKK turbocharger being added to the racer, the similarity ended there. Anyway, it provided the factory with an excellent piece of good PR just a couple of weeks before the new model was launched.

The other works 924 was a two-litre GTR model competing in the IMSA category. Wearing number 36, this was

A pensive-looking Helmuth Bott (right) in the Porsche pit. Bott was born in 1925, and worked for Mercedes and Bosch before joining Porsche in 1951. He moved to the Experimental Department three years later, becoming the head of R&D in 1971. Standing beside him is Porsche stalwart, Peter Falk.

driven by Schurti and Rouse (two of the drivers from the 1980 campaign), but gearbox problems resulted in the car finishing no higher than 11th overall and fourth in Class.

The third 924 was a private entry – a Group 4 924 GTR entered by the Eminence Racing Team, and driven by the Almeras brothers and Sivel. Sadly, they were dogged by problems (they had to change the gearbox only two hours into the event), and retired just four hours later.

Jacky Ickx and Derek Bell won for the Stuttgart marque, incidentally,

Walter Rohrl at work in the 924 GTP, actually a prototype for the forthcoming 944, although it would be some time before a turbocharged version reached the marketplace. This vehicle, apart from the engine (which produced 420bhp at 6800rpm), had similar running gear to the 924 GTR.

Left: The 924 Carrera GTR of Schurti and Rouse being chased down by a Lancia. Both GTRs eventually succumbed to gearbox problems.

Right: Getting Barth settled in his seat after Rohrl (still in his helmet, to the left) finishes yet another stint behind the wheel.

Right: The works-entered 924 GTP driven by Jurgen Barth and Walter Rohrl was the only front-engined Porsche to finish Le Mans in 1981.

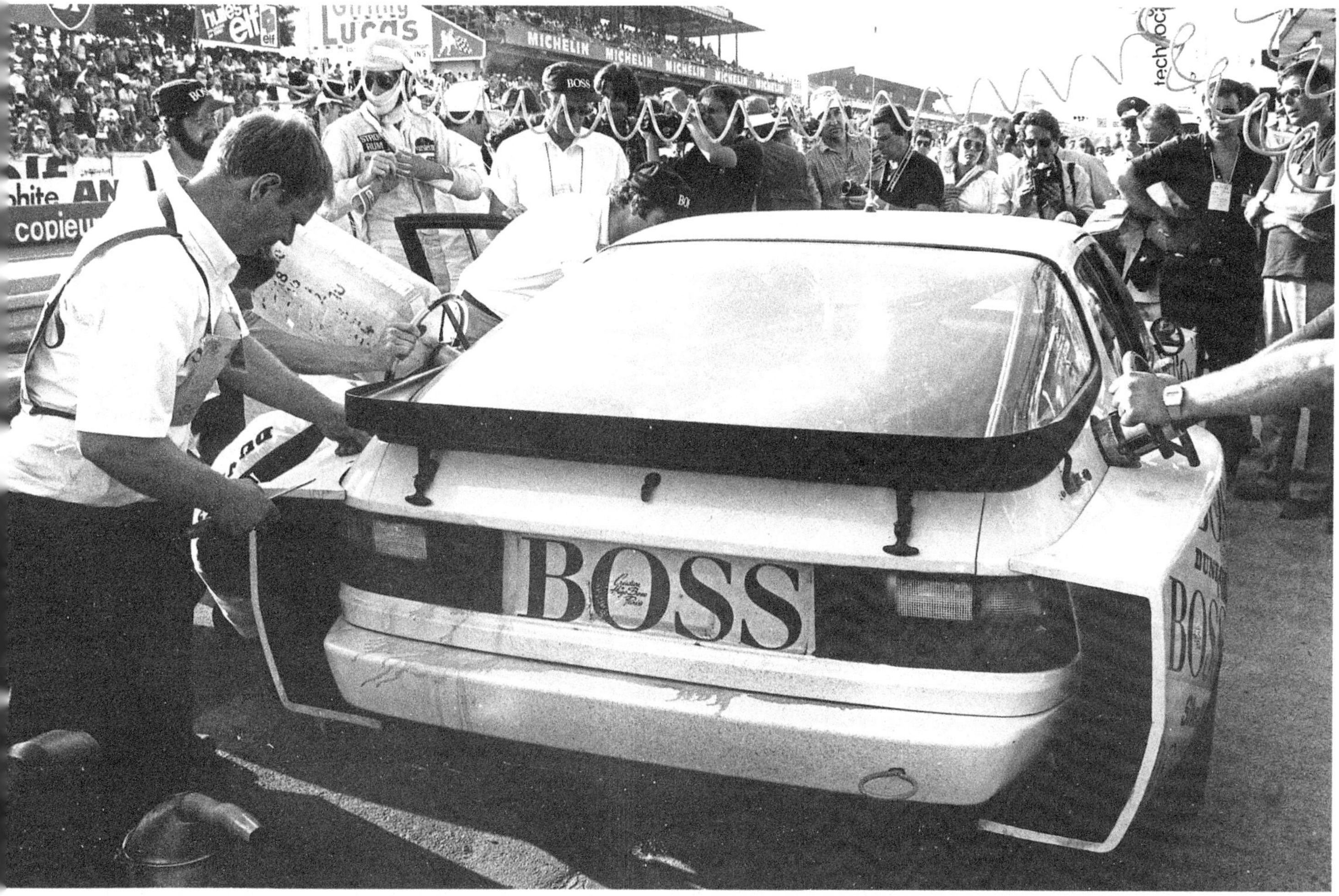
Lucas
elf
MICHELIN
BOSS

Barth
Rohrl
1
BOSS
DUNLOP
Shell
BOSCH
TELETRON
BILSTEIN

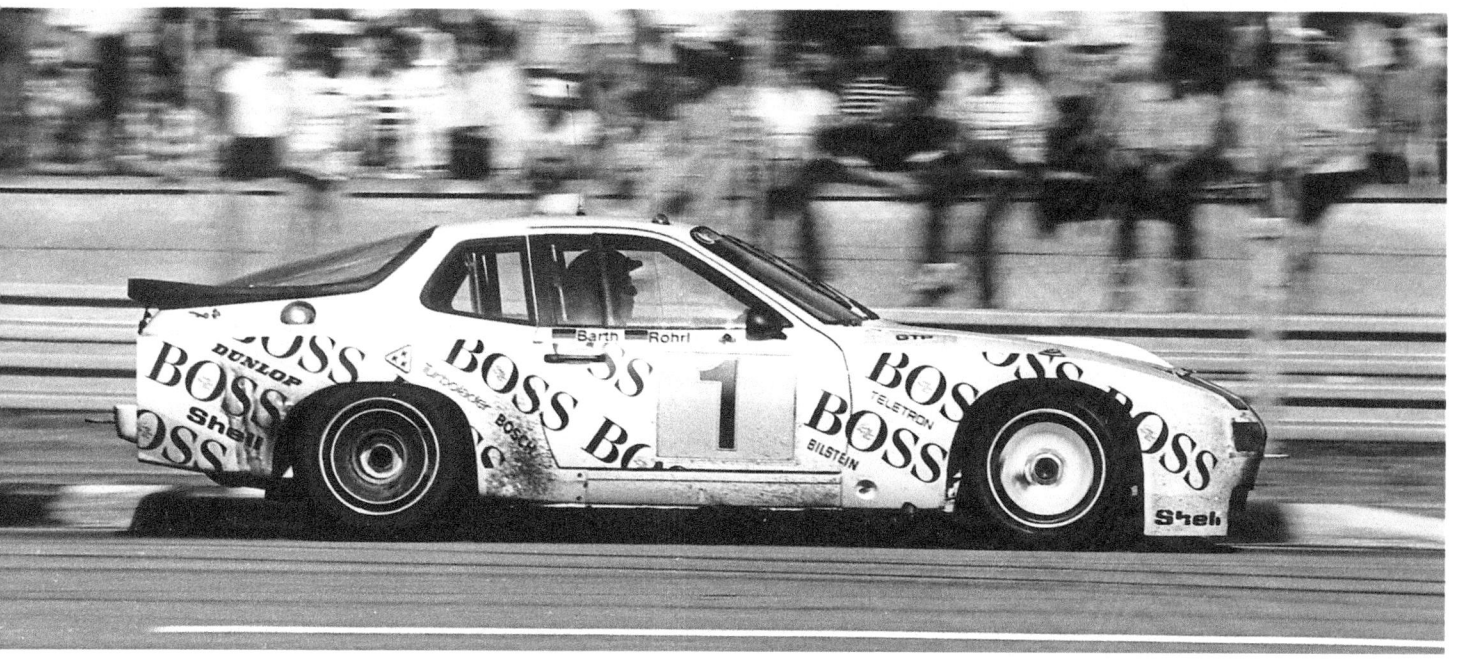

Walter Rohrl with his works-prepared 924 Carrera GTS rally car, pictured alongside a rather more standard-looking 924 Turbo.

Rohrl and Geistdorfer on the 1981 Metz Rally. Almeras, who had experience with the type in Monte Carlo, helped develop the car.

The Barth/Kussmaul car entered on the 1982 Monte Carlo Rally graced the cover of Rally Sport magazine. The pair finished tenth overall, second in Group B. Ironically, the event was won by Rohrl and Geistdorfer in an Opel.

RALLY SPORT

March 1982 UK 60p IR 84p (inc VAT)

Rallying Supercars – what will it mean to the clubman?

Basic Handling – A Black Art Explained

Win a trip to Ypres

guiding a Group 6 936 to an easy victory, 14 laps ahead of its nearest rival; this was Ickx's record-breaking fifth win at Le Mans.

Rally update

Things had been quiet on the rallying front for a while, but then the Barth/Kussmaul pairing appeared on the 1981 Monte Carlo Rally, the first event on the 1981 WRC calender. Starting at number 32, sadly, their Group 4 924 Turbo (registration LB-NW 317) retired about 400 miles from the end with transmission problems. However, they were still classified as finishers, so from 263 starters, they ended the classic in 96th place.

The 1981 Tour de Corse, which started on 30 April, signified the debut of the 924 Carrera GTS on a WRC event. A French-prepared car was entered by Jacques Almeras (race number 19, registration S-EK 2805), but he had a number of minor problems before an accident finally led to retirement.

Just over a month later, the 1980 World Champion, Walter Rohrl, gave the works-prepared 924 Carrera GTS its first outing. Porsche decided to enter the Hessen Rally (a round of the European Championship), and with Mercedes withdrawing from the WRC, Rohrl, who had signed a contract with the Stuttgart team, was without a drive. Who could be better? Walter Rohrl and Christian Geistdorfer justified their number one starting position and took S-EK 8747 to an easy victory, giving Porsche its first works rally team win in many years.

As well as providing Rohrl with the GTS for a number of other European rallies (he won three), Porsche later gave him a works-prepared 911SC for the San Remo Rally, marking the first official Porsche entry on a WRC event since 1978.

The turbocharged 924 Carrera GTS was far from ideal for rallying, with little power under 5000rpm and relatively slow gearchanges due to the lengthy selector on the transaxle. But as Rohrl later said: "We only did six rallies [with the GTS], though each time the car improved. If only we'd used it three or four more times, it could have been an excellent rally car."

133

A rear view of the 1982 Monte Carlo Rally machine.

Inset: Andy Rouse drove in all three 924 Le Mans entries. A gifted driver/engineer, and a gentleman, the author was lucky enough to meet him on many occasions, as his old Coventry workshop was situated just down the road from the author's house.

The Busby/Bundy 924 Carrera GTR, which finished 16th overall, 87 laps down on the winning Porsche. It's seen here being followed by the Rouse/Lloyd machine.

Derek Bell helped develop the Carrera GT, but won Le Mans in a 936 in 1981 and a 956 in 1982. On both occasions, he was partnered by Jacky Ickx – a formidable combination.

BF Goodrich advertising following its successful 1982 Le Mans campaign. It was the only car in the entire field to finish on road-legal tyres!

Another tyre manufacturer took to the 924 model; Hankook sponsored a one-make racing series in the mid-1990s.

its withdrawal, Rohrl duly signed for Opel.

Thankfully, the 924 was destined to make a few more appearances. On the 1981 Ivory Coast Rally, the privateer ladies team of Marianne Hoepfner and 'Biche' entered a French-registered 924, but they retired early with distributor trouble. Incidentally, 'Biche' (otherwise known as Michele Petit) was Jean-Claude Andruet's co-driver when he won the very first WRC round, the 1973 Monte Carlo Rally.

The 1982 Monte was the 100th WRC event, and Barth and Kussmaul finished tenth in their French-registered 924 Carrera GTS. The German pair led Group B for a while, but it was Jean-Pierre Ballet in a 911SC who eventually took Group B honours, just one place ahead of Barth on the road. A little later in the year, Jacky Ickx took the wheel of a Gitanes-sponsored Group 4 924 Carrera GTS in the Boucles de Spa. Sadly, the highly-successful WSC driver was to retire on this occasion.

1982 Le Mans

1982 was the year in which the Group C gladiators entered the scene, so the all-new 956 did tend to overshadow the less glamorous 924s. BF Goodrich, the tyre manufacturer, entered a 924 GTR to compete in the IMSA/GTO category. Wearing race number 87 and driven by Jim Busby and Doc Bundy, it finished first in Class and 16th overall, after completing 2307.9 miles at an average speed of 96.2mph.

The other two GTRs, both in the IMSA/GTO category (although only

However, after the appearance of the 944, the programme gradually fizzled out. The main reason, though, was not the 944, but the new Group system due for introduction in 1982. With the birth of the Group B supercars, the face – and pace – of

rallying was changing, and changing fast. Perhaps rightly, in view of the availability of the stunning Quattro (developed by Walter Tresor under contract number EA-262), it was decided to leave the WRC competition cars to Audi. With Porsche declaring

two-litres, the turbo made them 2.8s in the eyes of the FIA, and thus GTO, i.e. GT Over 2.5 litres), failed to finish.

Car 84 was entered by GTi Engineering and sponsored by Canon, but even with the experienced Andy Rouse and Richard Lloyd behind the wheel, they would not reach the end, being disqualified in the sixth hour whilst lying in 23rd place.

Number 86, a sister car to Bundy's machine, was driven by Kemper Miller, Pat Bedard and Manfred Schurti, but this vehicle was destined to retire halfway through the event.

There were no 924s at Le Mans in 1983, but there was a surprise appearance of a 928S, which eventually finished 22nd overall. Another 928 arrived at the Sarthe track the following year, coming in 20th overall. At least it made a change from the scores of 956s and 911-based machines.

A return to F1

After a few outings towards the end of 1983, the Porsche-built, 1.5-litre, turbocharged TAG engine won the first race of the 1984 Formula One season and, combined with the McLaren chassis, the twin-turbo V6 went on to dominate for the rest of the year.

The commission had originally come in 1981. The TAG engine project was financed completely by the massive Techniques d'Avant Garde concern, and although Hans Mezger was responsible for its development, the specification was basically laid down by McLaren. Only a tiny 'Made by Porsche' label proclaimed its source, but there is no doubt that Porsche benefited from its success.

Excellent results came in 1984 and 1985 (by which time the unit was pushing out the best part of 1000bhp), but the Honda era had well and truly arrived the following season – although Prost won the Drivers' Championship, Williams-Honda won the constructors' title by a convincing margin.

While all of this motorsport activity was going on, development of the 924 continued unabated. The next chapter returns to where chapter four left off, with the start of the 1981 model year.

PORSCHE 924

6

THE TWILIGHT YEARS

The 924 had now established itself, a long list of developments since introduction helping to improve the vehicle year after year. But the strong deutschmark was still a problem, especially in the States where people were accustomed to paying much less for automobiles than their European counterparts. While sales were still relatively strong in 1979, with US dealers selling no less than 8345 924s (635 of which were the expensive Turbo models), this was followed by a very poor 1980. Total Porsche sales dropped by 25% – around 3500 normally-aspirated models found new homes, along with 1925 Turbos. Anyway, another series of refinements were in the pipeline ...

The 1981 model year

For the 1981 model year, a number of changes were applied to the 924 range. From August 1980 production, repeater indicators were fitted on the front wings, yet more sound insulation was added (including carpeting to the centre console), the door cappings featured embossed 'Porsche' script, and there was a new stalk design on the steering column.

On the Turbo, in addition to the foregoing modifications, the fuel tank on European specification cars now had a capacity of 18.5 gallons (84 litres), the 360mm diameter four-spoke steering wheel became standard, and gauge markings reverted to a more traditional white on black (instead of the green on black previously used). But the biggest differences were under the bonnet.

A 1981 model year 924 for the home market. Note the repeater indicator mounted on the front wing.

Another view of the same car. For 1981, normally-aspirated models came with the bigger 14.5 gallon (66 litre) fuel tank, similar to that previously fitted to the Turbo.

The engine now featured an 8.5:1 compression ratio and better crankcase breathing, and came equipped with a smaller turbocharger unit to improve response, along with a Siemens-Hartig fully-electronic digital ignition system. This reduced fuel consumption and emission levels, whilst at the same time enhancing power output – now up 7bhp to 177 at 5500rpm, with peak torque being quoted as 184lbft at 3500rpm (an improvement of 4lbft at the same engine speed).

US models also acquired this modification, bringing with it a useful gain in power – 154bhp at 5500rpm, and 155lbft of torque at 3300rpm –

these figures being almost identical to those of the Alfa Romeo GTV6. At last, American specification Turbos got rear disc brakes as standard, and came fitted with a new Audi 016G five-speed gearbox. This had fifth up and to the right, like the normally-aspirated cars, with revised ratios (3.60, 2.12, 1.46, 1.11 and 0.73:1 respectively) to suit a new 3.89:1 final-drive.

This transmission duly replaced the old 016 units in cars destined for Europe and the rest of the world. While the first four gears were the same, top gear was changed in the majority of countries to give 0.86:1, while the final-drive ratio was kept at 3.89:1.

Road & Track carried out an interesting comparison test, repeating one from 1976 when it pitted the 924 against its Alfa Romeo and Datsun competitors. This time it was between the 924 Turbo, the V6 version of the Alfa GTV and the 280ZX Turbo – the top developments of each model.

The Porsche was by far the most expensive, with the list price running to $21,500. This was around $4500 more than the Milanese beauty, and $5000 up on the well-equipped Japanese vehicle. While the European cars were very similar in terms of power and performance, the Datsun showed a distinct advantage off the mark,

Standard coachwork colours (1981 MY)

Mocha Black, Colorado Beige, Guards Red, Venus Red, Monaco Blue, Mauritius Blue, Conifer Green, Alpine White, Havana Brown.

Special coachwork colours

Pewter Metallic, Black Metallic, Minerva Blue Metallic, Indiana Red Metallic, Saturn Metallic, Meteor Metallic, Onyx Metallic, Diamond Silver Metallic.

Dual tone colours

Colorado Beige over Mocha Black, Pewter Metallic over Havana Brown, Inari Silver Metallic over Onyx Metallic, Diamond Silver Metallic over Meteor Metallic.

Trim materials

Black, Brown or Beige leatherette with matching inlays. Alternatively, inlays could be in a chequered Pasha velour (Grey/Black or Beige/Brown), or Pinstripe velour (Black with White or Brown with Beige); seat facings could also be supplied in Grey/Black or Beige/Brown Berber cloth, or Black, Brown or Beige leather as an option. Carpets came in Black, Brown or Beige.

Front view of the 1981 model year 924 Turbo. Panel fit was generally good, although the gaps were rather big by modern standards.

Chassis of the 1981 Turbo, the engine now producing a healthy 177bhp.

although fell behind in the handling department. Ultimately, it was the Alfa that scored a convincing victory, regardless of price.

Turbos destined for American shores now featured air conditioning and electric windows as standard (electrically-adjustable mirrors, then a $220 option, would also become standard the following year).

In the UK, which continued to be Porsche's second biggest export market, the price of the standard 924 was initially unchanged at £9104, despite carrying a new full seven-year bodywork warranty (it had previously been six years, already an outstanding guarantee); the Lux was £9582, with the automatic adding a further £478.

Meanwhile, the 924 Turbo was a hefty £13,998.

Bill Boddy of *Motor Sport* tried the 924 Turbo in the opening months of 1981. He noted: "There is a fine air of restrained good taste about the 924 as a whole, yet it possesses such enjoyable performance and road manners as to make one go out just for the sheer pleasure of driving it ... in my book the 924 Turbo justifies the term 'thoroughbred'."

Regarding the modified power unit, the *Autocar* said: "The engine gives excellent response, making overtaking swift and safe ... The only short-coming is the usual delay for the turbocharger to begin to respond, and although this is less than before, it is still important to be in the right gear, enabling the engine revs to be on the right side of 2500rpm, for quick response to be available."

Paul Horrell drove one of the

Side view of the 1981 model year Turbo, this example carrying German registration plates.

Following a change in Federal regulations, from 1981, US specification cars were fitted with the same higher-powered halogen bulb headlights as European models. Formerly, the rules specified that only sealed beam headlamps (30% less powerful than halogen lights) could be used in the States.

177bhp models for *Supercar Classics* and observed: "Because of the way the car throws itself down the road at wide throttle openings, you soon have to shift up, and gearchanging is a continual task if you're to keep the engine in that happy rev band between no go and no peace.

"That's a shame, because the Getrag 'box is unco-operative. There's no spring to guide you between the two-three and four-five planes, and the synchros are slow. Double-declutching helps, but the layout of the pedals doesn't encourage it. Still, the clutch action is good and progressive, and the lever well-placed.

"There's often a mid-engined feel about the 924s. They wander slightly at the straight-ahead, the nose bobbing over surface ripples. Turn-in is instant and reassuring, slightly understeer-biased, the steering full of feel. Praise be for the absence of message-smothering power assistance.

"Commit yourself fully to a bend, though, and you find out where the motor is. The 924 has all the friendliness of the best front-engined cars. You can play with it, balance it on steering and throttle with impunity. The 924 defines its limits by a gentle relinquishing of grip, rather than a knife-edge propensity to swop ends."

With the same gearing as before, the *Autocar* managed to record a top speed of 144mph, with the standing-quarter coming up in just 15.7 seconds. These statistics were almost identical to those of the three-litre Maserati Merak, although the latter couldn't come near the 924's fuel consumption figure (an amazing 23.6mpg average), and it cost £5000 more into the bargain.

By February 1981, over 100,000 924s had been produced, making it one of the most successful Porsche models ever, and there was still a lot of development potential left in it. Shortly after, 400 'Weissach' limited edition

The 1981 MY 924 Turbo for the US market. Note the lack of repeater indicators on US models, deemed unnecessary with the side markers.

models were built for the American market, and these were followed by a '50th Jubilee' car in the summer. Finished in Pewter Metallic with a black interior, just over 1000 were built, most of them staying in Germany.

Meanwhile, back in Stuttgart, where the standard normally-aspirated 924 was now priced at DM29,530 (DM13,250 less than the Turbo), a lot of political wrangling was going on.

Corporate matters

Ernst Fuhrmann, Porsche's Chairman and the designer of the first Carrera engine, was eventually ousted from office in November 1980. Ferry Porsche

Interior of the American specification Turbo; it could also be equipped with the smaller, four-spoke steering wheel that was now standard for Europe. Note the green numerals on gauges, which were changed to white for production models, and the carpeting on the centre console, helping to give the cockpit an air of quality.

The 100,000th 924 was produced on 4 February 1981. The Stuttgart company had paid Volkswagen a royalty on all these cars as part of the deal to bring the EA-425 project back to Porsche.

Interior of the normally-aspirated 924 for 1981.

later stated he felt Fuhrmann had trouble understanding the market (he did come from an engineering rather than commercial background, after all), but there was a definite underlying personality clash.

Peter Schutz became Chairman on 1 January 1981, hand-picked by Ferry Porsche. Born in Berlin in 1930, Schutz had spent most of his life in America before moving to the Deutz concern in 1978 to take up a position as Director of Powertrain R&D.

Whereas Fuhrmann had almost dismissed the 911 in recent years, preferring to put the company's resources into the 928 and the forthcoming 944, Schutz made it his mission to revive the legendary model and give it the development needed to keep it competitive. It was exactly what Porsche enthusiasts wanted to hear.

Schutz also made his position on the 924 plain: "I appreciate this dispute

over what a real Porsche is or isn't. But to make it very clear – if the name Porsche appears on all the different models then it means they were all designed, built, and offered by Porsche. For me that is the only real Porsche. A little bit less real doesn't exist.

"Our goal is to offer the full range of technical possibilities as well as driving sensations. Therefore, it's unthinkable to neglect any segment of our range of models."

Across at Volkswagen, the Scirocco gained a facelifted body in March 1981 (designed in-house this time by Herbert Schafer), and, about

Peter W. Schutz – Porsche's new Chairman.

a year later, Toni Schmucker was replaced as head of the company by Carl Horst Hahn, whose family had a long tradition in the German motor industry (his father had been a director of the DKW concern).

The 944

The gap between the 924 and 928 was narrowed for the 1982 model year by

the appearance of the 2.5 litre, four-cylinder 944. Although clearly based on the 924 both visually (there was a striking resemblance to the Carrera GT) and in mechanical layout, the 944 used less VW-Audi sourced parts, and was much quicker.

Although the 928 went into production with a 4.5 litre V8, the plans for the original engine proposed

Although Schutz was determined to save the 911, the future of the 924 also looked assured.

The 944 as it appeared at the 1981 Frankfurt Show.

Consumer Orientation
No. 17 in a Series
of Technical Papers
Subject: Prüfstrecke.
The Porsche Proving Grounds
at Weissach.

17 Porsche 924/924 Turbo

A computer can build a car, but it can not build a Porsche. Because while a computer can provide quantitative data, it can not make qualitative decisions on the pertinent factors—such as optimum vehicle responsiveness and handling characteristics— that make only a Porsche a Porsche. These are best determined under actual driving conditions, by men with years of experience, using the legendary Porsche racers as the standard. At the Weissach Prüfstrecke, we turn cars into Porsches.

The Porsche Proving Grounds are an integral part of the Porsche Research and Development Center at Weissach. Thus, the engineers who design the cars, the mechanics who build the prototypes, and the technicians who conduct the extensive laboratory tests can easily test-drive the cars under a myriad of operating conditions.

The proving grounds include a 1.57-mile high-speed Can-Am course. A narrower, twisting Berg Kurs (Mountain Course) with S-bends, hairpin turns, and Alpine hills. Special surfaces, including bumps, potholes, cobblestones, water trough, and jump ramp. Three skid pads. And a dirt track. Whatever the track, whatever the test, the objective is the same: to create the optimum high-performance car.

On the Can-Am course, Porsche perfected turbocharging for cars—by solving the problem of poor throttle response—and developed the 917 Turbo Can-Am champion, the 936 Turbo LeMans champion, and the 924 Turbo street car. Like the 917 and the 936, the 924 has the unique Porsche bypass valve system.

Thus, on demand, following deceleration (for example, during gear shifting or braking), boost is available again in only 0.1 second.

On the Berg Kurs, Porsche perfected the transaxle—a proven racing design—for the 924 street cars. It places the engine in front and transmission in back and produces a nearly-perfect 50-50 front-to-rear weight distribution for balanced braking and improved cornering. And it creates a high polar moment of inertia that reduces pitching and increases directional control.

On the skid pad, Porsche optimized the 924's handling characteristics. For example, on a 65-ft radius curve at 30 mph, the 924 generates 0.85g lateral acceleration.

For 1982, many new features, including air conditioning and electrically heated outside mirrors, have been added as standard equipment to the 924 and 924 Turbo, making them even better values than they have been in the past. At Porsche, we optimize not only performance, but also value. Call toll-free: (800) 447-4700. In Illinois, (800) 322-4400.

PORSCHE + AUDI
NOTHING EVEN COMES CLOSE

The 924 soldiered on into the US 1982 model year line-up, but only briefly until the 944 arrived. All cars now came with air conditioning and electrically-adjustable mirrors as standard.

a five-litre unit. Basically, the 944 powerplant was half of that prototype V8. With a 2479cc displacement, it developed a healthy 163bhp, contra-rotating balance shafts helping to keep it smooth.

Writing for *Classic Cars*, Roger Bell noted at the time of the new model's UK launch: "So excellent are the qualities that really matter – performance, economy, refinement, comfort, build quality, finish – that the 944's few deficiencies seem rather trivial ... Even at £13,000, the five-speed manual does not appear to have a competitor in sight."

The 1982 model year
Compared to vehicles like the best-selling RX-7, the 924 – at almost $17,000 in basic trim – was far too

The 924 (left) and 924 Turbo for the American 1982 model year. Incidentally, a total of 5845 Turbos were sold in the States – about 46% of the total production run.

Rear of the US specification 924 for 1982. By the spring, the 924 series had been replaced in America by the new 944 model.

Right, below: Publicity shot of the 1982 MY normally-aspirated 924.

expensive in the USA, pricing itself out of the market. To sell it any cheaper would have meant little or no profit, so after a few months, the 944 – which gave a better return – was the only four-cylinder Porsche listed for America's 1982 MY, arriving there in spring and sold as an early 1983 model.

Supplies of 924 engines were running low anyway, so these were used for Europe where sales were still steady, especially in the British Isles. Prices in the UK were unchanged from 1981, although the cars were given detail improvements once again.

The heater was upgraded

(although judging by press comment, one would hardly notice), the roof was strengthened to enable the 'Porsche Carrier System' to be fitted, there was a Porsche badge on the glovebox, and the three-spoke steering wheel became standard.

In July 1982, production of the 924 Turbo officially ceased, although some were produced for the Italian market until the end of 1983 (including a limited run of 88 cars finished in Zermatt Silver Metallic), where the exorbitant tax on vehicles

The European (German-registered) 924 and 924 Turbo (right) for 1982. The same cars were used in the Japanese catalogue for that year.

Standard coachwork colours (1982 MY)

Mocha Black, Gabon Grey, Guards Red, Gambia Red, Mauritius Blue, Alpine White, Havana Brown.

Special coachwork colours

Pewter Metallic, Light Blue Metallic, Black Metallic, Ocean Green Metallic, Claret Metallic, Meteor Metallic, Diamond Silver Metallic.

Dual tone colours

Alpine White over Gabon Grey, Pewter Metallic over Havana Brown, Diamond Silver Metallic over Meteor Metallic.

Trim materials

Black, Brown or Beige leatherette with matching inlays. Alternatively, inlays could be in a chequered Pasha velour (Grey/Black or Beige/Brown), or Pinstripe velour (Black with White or Brown with Beige); seat facings could also be supplied in Beige/White or Brown/White Berber cloth, or Black, Brown or Beige leather as an option. Carpets came in Black, Brown or Beige.

Interior of the same car with the rear seats folded to give extra luggage space.

944 was £13,390 at this time.

At the start of 1983, while most manufacturers were struggling (Volkswagen made heavy losses in 1982 and 1983), Porsche was booming. The Zuffenhausen works was building around 75 cars a day (55 911s to 20 928Ss), while the Neckarsulm factory (which was still rented from Volkswagen) was producing about 105 – 80 944s and 25 924s.

Schutz was fulfilling his promise to revive the 911, a Cabriolet version

with engines over two-litres made it a viable proposition. UK sales of the Turbo totalled 905 units, incidentally, or 980, if the Carrera GT is included.

Meanwhile, for Switzerland, Italy and the home market, a number of small, limited edition runs had been produced based on the normally-aspirated 924.

The 1983 model year

Inside the car, money was being saved via a revised vinyl door trim. The 'Porsche' script on the door cappings had long since gone, and door pockets were finished with carpet. The end result looked bare and quite strange – especially if the cockpit was trimmed in black – to be perfectly honest. The other major change was the adoption of a rear spoiler as standard, the latter having been listed as an option for the first time the previous year.

Rear view of the 1982 car, seen here with optional spoiler. The latter would become a standard fitment for the 1983 model year.

As for prices, although the standard 924 was still listed, it is perhaps better to quote £9993 for the 924 Lux (automatic transmission was £499 extra on both models); the new

having been shown at the 1982 Geneva Show, while in 1983, the range acquired a new 3164cc engine. With 231bhp on tap (a jump of 27bhp over the already increased 1980 outputs),

Tasteful advertising from the UK, this piece dating from spring 1982.

Engine bay of the 924.

Right, top: Another view of the 1983 model year 924, now sporting a rear spoiler as standard. This slightly reduced drag, and most seem to feel it also improves the appearance of the car. Personally, the author would do without it – the original shape is much cleaner.

The 924 for the 1983 model year. Although the overall design had changed very little since the car was introduced in 1975, the lines still looked very fresh and modern.

British advertising from 1983, making the most of the 924's assault on Le Mans.

A 1984 model year 924 at speed on the open roads of Germany.

Rear view of the same car. The sunroof was now the same as that fitted to the 944, featuring an electric tilt facility.

The 1984 model year

The big news for Porsche fans was the introduction of the four-wheel drive 959 supercar, first shown at the 1983 Frankfurt Show. The twin-turbo, 2.9 litre engine produced no less

Comparing this picture with one from 1976, it is easy to appreciate how much the interior had improved through a series of detail changes. This German-registered car has the smaller, four-spoke steering wheel, and a Blaupunkt stereo radio/cassette. Note the Porsche badge on the glovebox.

these models were given the Carrera appellation, a perfect complement to the 3.3 litre Turbo. The standard 928 was dropped in the reshuffle, with the 928S carrying the mantle for the series.

It was around this time that Dr Helmut Kohl replaced Helmut Schmidt as Germany's Chancellor (basically, head of the German government). The latter had done a sterling job in bringing the country through a series of oil shocks and currency crises, although unemployment continued to rise during the 1980s. An interesting development was the rise of the Greens (an environmentalist party), as the car was a major target for criticism: what would this mean for the future?

than 450bhp, endowing the Group B monster with a 0-60 time of 3.9 seconds and a top speed approaching 200mph. However, only 200 were made, and for mere mortals who couldn't find the DM420,000 (ten times the price of a 944!) necessary to secure one, the 924 was now being fitted with the electric sunroof from the 944 (if the sunroof option was specified), and also gained an electric release button for the rear hatch; the switch was situated on the centre console.

Judging by the long list of options, and the relatively high base price, it's easy to see why 924 sales were steady rather than brisk. While the RX-7 wasn't as cheap in the UK as it was in America, and the threat from the Datsun 280ZX was about to end as the model went further upmarket (although the attractive new Silvia would soon take its place), the Ford Capri 2.8i, with its 130mph performance, represented an absolute bargain. Cars like the Opel Manta GTE, VW Scirocco GTi, Audi Coupé, Lancia Beta Coupé VX and Renault Fuego Turbo offered performance on a budget; the Toyota Supra gave a lot more muscle and a far higher specification for similar money, and then there were slightly more expensive alternatives like the Lotus range and the three-door Saab Turbo SE, but add a few extras to the 924 and the difference was soon obviated.

There was certainly a lot of competition on the market, and even stronger rivals would continue to filter through as the years progressed. As a matter of interest, the five-speed

UK price list – September 1983

924 Coupé	£10,879.86
924 Coupé three-speed Automatic	£11,369.47
924 Lux Coupé	£11,495.31
924 Lux Coupé three-speed Automatic	£11,984.92

Standard UK specification includes:

Coupé
Five-speed manual transmission
Light alloy 6J x 14 road wheels with 185/70 HR14 tyres
Front anti-roll bar
Additional driving lamps mounted in front bumper
High intensity rear fog lamps
Heated rear window
Two-speed windscreen wipers, intermittent wipe setting and electrically-operated windscreen washers
Leather covered sport steering wheel (380mm diameter)
Lockable fuel filler cap
Driver's door mirror – mechanically adjustable from interior
Rear compartment luggage cover
Electrically-operated rear hatch release

Lux Coupé (in addition to the above equipment)
Electrically-operated door windows
Tinted, heat insulating glass
Rear window wiper
Headlamp washers
Electrically-heated and adjustable driver's door mirror

Optional equipment

Light alloy 6J x 15 road wheels with anti-theft device – multi-spoked appearance - with 205/60 HR15 low-profile tyres and rear wheelarch trim	£556.89
Front and rear anti-roll bars (large diameter)	£98.42
Front and rear anti-roll bars (large diameter) with sport shock absorbers	£260.38
Limited-slip differential (manual transmission only)	£459.71
Rear window wiper (standard equipment on Lux Coupé)	£169.43
High pressure headlamp washers (standard equipment on Lux Coupé)	£132.05
Electrically-heated and adjustable driver's door mirror (standard equipment on Lux Coupé)	£68.52
Electrically-heated and adjustable passenger door mirror (only available with above)	£105.89
Burglar alarm system	£149.50
Anti-theft device for wheels (locking bolt)	£36.13
Tinted, heat insulating glass (standard equipment on Lux Coupé)	£158.22
Removable sunroof panel with electric tilt facility	£560.63
Air conditioner (only available with tinted glass)	£959.30
National Panasonic digital self-seek stereo radio with combined auto-reverse stereo cassette player (10W per channel) with Dolby and metal tape facilities, four speakers and automatic electric aerial	£695.18
Stereo radio cassette player (as above) with manual aerial	£548.17
Automatic electric aerial with four speakers	£316.45
Manual aerial with four speakers	£169.43

(Continued overleaf ...)

UK price list – September 1983	
(Continued from previous page ...)	
Standard seats with 'Porsche' cloth seat inlays and bolsters – pair	£89.70
Leatherette sport seats with 'Porsche' cloth seat inlays – pair	£241.70
Leatherette sport seats with 'Porsche' cloth seat inlays and bolsters – pair	£331.40
Leather sport seats – pair	£877.07
Partial leather front seats (seat facings only)	£275.33
Electrically-operated door windows (standard equipment on Lux Coupé)	£297.76
Cloth door panel facings with velour check or pinstripe trim (only available with electric windows)	£68.52
Cassette and coin holder	£73.51
Metallic paint	£394.93
Deletion of rear spoiler	No charge

A British-registered 924. The multi-spoke 6J x 15 alloy wheels were a £557 option in 1984, and came fitted with 205/60 rubber; the mudguards on the rear wheelarches were part of the deal.

944 was priced at £15,309, while the 911 ranged from £21,464 to £33,878; the 928S S2, the only 928 available in Britain at the time, was listed at £30,679.

Fast Lane magazine compared the 924 with a Mazda RX-7. It pointed out that, although the Wankel-engined car was cheaper to buy initially, three years down the line, the Porsche had consistently retained a greater proportion of its price on the second-hand market. Having commented how difficult it was to split the two, the magazine concluded: "The complete

equation, then, just balances in favour of the 924: dynamically it has the edge and economically it's a shrewd bet, too."

Across the Atlantic, on 31 August 1984, the long-running marketing agreement which resulted in Porsches and Audis being sold alongside each other under the auspices of Volkswagen of America Inc., finally came to an end. From now on, Porsche was on its own, with offices in Reno and the new distribution system utilizing 40 so-called 'Porsche Centres' across the States.

For 1985, Americans received a 32v five-litre version of the 928S, rated at 288bhp. By summer 1986, this model was offered in all markets, now known as the Series 4 and with a useful 320bhp on tap, giving the luxury GT a top speed approaching 170mph.

End of the line – part I
Naturally, with production about to end, there were very few changes for 1985; the windscreen washer nozzles were now heated, and a graduated tint was added to the windscreen (previously an option). However, prices

Standard coachwork colours (1984 MY)
Black, Pasadena Yellow, Guards Red, Copenhagen Blue.

Special coachwork colours
Pewter Metallic, Ruby Red Metallic, Montego Black Metallic, Gemini Grey Metallic, Sable Brown Metallic, Sapphire Metallic, Light Bronze Metallic, Zermatt Silver Metallic.

Trim materials
Black, Brown or Grey-Beige leatherette with matching inlays. Alternatively, inlays could be in a chequered Pasha velour (Grey/Black or Grey-Beige/Brown), or Pinstripe velour (Black with White, Brown with Beige or Grey-Beige with White); seat facings could also be supplied in Black, Brown or Grey-Beige 'Porsche' cloth or leather as an option. Carpets came in Black, Brown, Grey-Beige or Grey.

The 1985 model year 924.

Standard coachwork colours (1985 MY)
Black, Pastel Beige, Guards Red, Copenhagen Blue, Alpine White.

Special coachwork colours
Graphite Metallic, Garnet Red Metallic, Kalahari Metallic, Stone Grey Metallic, Crystal Green Metallic, Sapphire Metallic, Mahogany Metallic, Zermatt Silver Metallic.

Trim materials
Black, Brown, Burgundy or Light Grey leatherette with matching inlays. Alternatively, inlays could be in Pinstripe velour (Black with White, Brown with Beige, Burgundy with White or Grey with White); seat facings could also be supplied in Pinstripe flannel cloth (in the same shades as the velour inlays), Black, Brown, Burgundy or Light Grey 'Porsche' cloth or leather as an option. Carpets came in Black, Brown, Burgundy or Grey.

once again rose significantly. The 924 Lux was now quoted at £12,123 (the automatic gearbox option adding a further £490). By the end of August, when the two-litre 924 last appeared on price lists, its retail price had gone up yet again to £12,837.

A total of 8630 normally-aspirated 924s had been sold in the UK by the

The Porsche line-up for 1985 (clockwise from the back): the 911 Turbo, the 911 Carrera in Cabriolet, Targa and coupé guise, the 928S, the 944, and the 924. This was the final year of the original 924, but it had lasted the best part of a decade and proved itself worthy of the Porsche name.

time production ended in July 1985. The much-talked about small Porsche, intended to slot into the range below the 924 (and possibly available in coupé, convertible and Targa form), simply failed to materialize. However, in Europe at least there was now a new 924-based model on the scene – the 924S.

7

THE 924 MAKES
A COMEBACK

The Stuttgart company was faced with two major problems in the mid-1980s: the short supply of Audi-built powerplants, and Germany's proposed new emissions regulations. With so many cars staying in Germany for home market consumption, the latter was just as important to Porsche as changes in Federal requirements for the majority of sports car manufacturers.

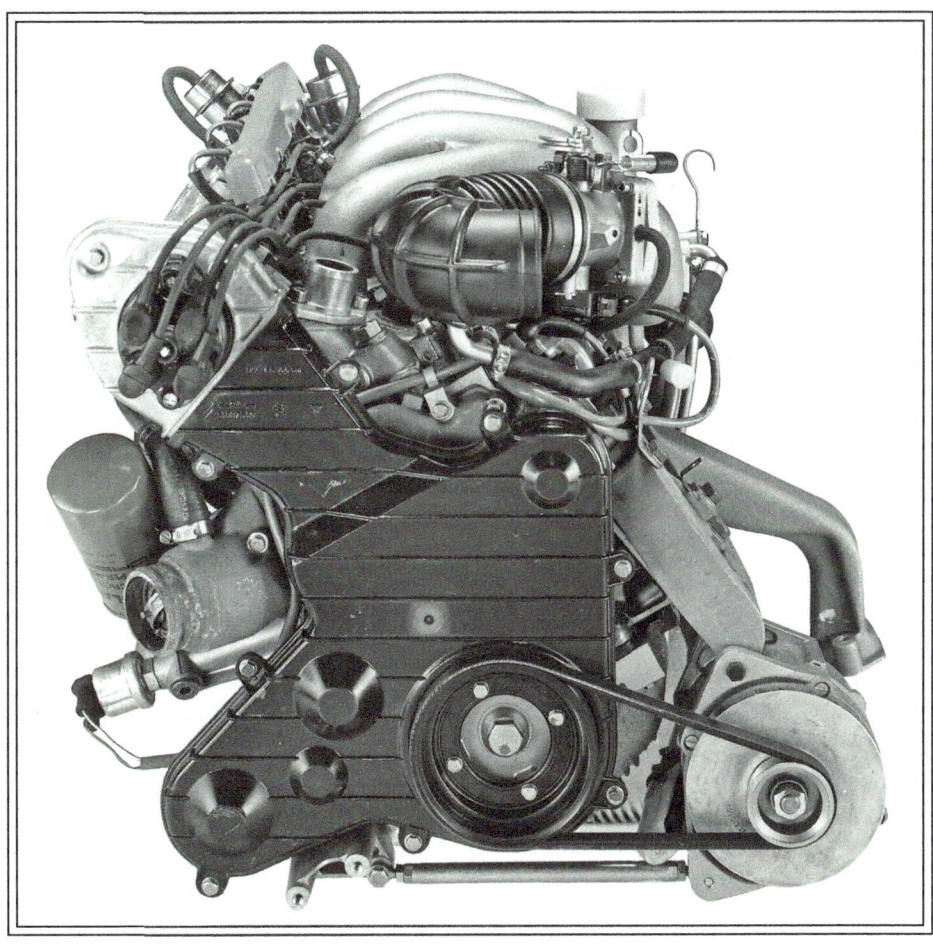

The 944 engine was adopted for the 924 in 1985. The balance shafts were positioned where the two smaller circular protrusions appear on the timing cover.

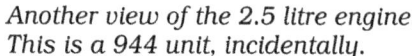

Another view of the 2.5 litre engine. This is a 944 unit, incidentally.

It had been speculated for some time that the 924 would continue in one form or another, some suggesting that it would be powered by a two-litre version of the 944 engine, others predicting the possibility of another Audi-based unit, perhaps even the fuel-injected 2.1 litre five-cylinder powerplant.

In the end, Porsche decided to keep the 944 lump as it was, albeit with a few minor modifications. At 2.5 litres, it would silence the critics who still delighted in making references to van engines, and give the 924 a new lease of life; but therein lay a problem.

The 924 was both lighter and cleaner through the air (with the rear spoiler, the 924 had a Cd of 0.34 compared to 0.35 for the 944), so with the same power, the 924 would have been faster than its more expensive stablemate, and that simply couldn't be allowed to happen. For that reason, power was reduced slightly in order to keep the 944 ahead in the performance stakes.

The bore and stroke of 100 x 78.9mm was retained, resulting in a displacement of 2479cc. The forged steel crankshaft ran in five main bearings in a two-piece light alloy block, while the single overhead-camshaft operated a single inlet and exhaust valve via hydraulic tappets in the aluminium alloy crossflow head; as with the 924 unit, a toothed belt was used to drive the camshaft.

Perhaps the most interesting feature was the use of two contra-rotating balance shafts, something invented by the forgotten genius, Dr Frederick Lanchester, at the turn of the century, but more recently employed by Mitsubishi for its Sigma engine. Running at twice the crankshaft speed, these guaranteed smooth engine operation despite the rather large capacity for a four-cylinder unit.

Clearly based on the 928 V8, the Porsche-designed powerplant was equipped with Bosch L-Jetronic fuel-injection, electric fuel pumps getting the petrol from the 14.5 gallon (66 litre) tank. A compression ratio of 9.7:1 would have meant a definite need for high octane fuel a few years earlier,

but with the modern digital electronic ignition, this high c/r didn't present a problem on the 91 octane (leaded or unleaded) grade specified. (Due to a different piston crown shape, the 944 was running at 10.6:1 at this time, which called for 95 octane petrol.)

The water-cooled unit, which developed 150bhp in the 924 application, was canted over 30 degrees to the right to keep the bonnet line as low as possible. The radiator was a sealed unit, employing a separate plastic header tank, while a thermostatically-controlled electric fan reduced noise and a needless drain on engine power.

The alternator was a larger 90 Amp unit, and although the 944 engine was longer than that of the 924's, the extensive use of alloys helped keep weight down. Indeed, the 944's four was just 73lbs (33kg) heavier. Powered by this 2.5 litre unit, the 924 was called the 924S.

The 924S

Introduced in Germany at DM41,950 (which represented a massive 21% increase over the outgoing two-litre 924), the 924S's Frankfurt Show debut was somewhat overshadowed by the recently-introduced 944 Turbo, and a surprise appearance from the 944 Cabriolet prototype. Although it would be some time before the latter model went into production, there's no doubt that it stole a lot of the 924S's thunder.

The engine (given the M44 designation), was by far the biggest change in the transformation from

The 944 power unit neatly installed in the 924 engine bay. The new model created by this combination was christened the 924S.

924 to 924S. As noted earlier, instead of developing 163bhp as it did in the 944, it was detuned to give 150bhp at 5800rpm and 144lbft of torque at 3000rpm. Interestingly, the power unit gave 150bhp on leaded or unleaded fuel, the latter being necessary with Germany's catalytic converter-equipped models.

To go with the new powerplant, the transmission was naturally sourced from the 944, the five-speed gearbox being a development of the Audi 016-based unit (carrying the 016J appellation, the shift pattern had fifth

Interior of the 924S for mainland Europe.

The rear seats. Note the 'Porsche' script running through the inlay material, and the luggage blind pulled over to hide the boot's contents.

Side view of the new 924S. The new wheels quickly identified the larger-engined car, but careful inspection also revealed that the rain gutters on the A-post and along the edge of the roof had been deleted.

Instrument faces were changed, with large white numerals. A three-spoke steering wheel was standard, although the smaller, four-spoke item was optional.

Two buttons on top of the backrests were released to fold the back seats. This was a more professional-looking arrangement than the cheap, flimsy-feeling pull-to-release straps fitted to earlier cars. For 1988, a split rear seat could be specified for an extra £350.

up and to the right, outside the 'H'), while the three-speed automatic was a suitably uprated version of the old O-87 'box. Power was taken to the transaxle via a hydraulically-operated clutch and 25mm diameter shaft supported by three bearings, *a la* 924 Turbo.

Gearing on the manual car was subtly different to that on the 924, with the ratios being 3.60, 2.12, 1.46, 1.07 and 0.83:1 respectively, mated to a 3.89:1 final-drive. This gave intermediate speeds of 34, 56, 81 and 111mph, with the factory quoting a maximum of 133mph; the 0-60 yardstick was said to be covered in 8.5 seconds, although independent tests would prove both of these figures to be typically conservative.

The suspension came from the latest version of the 944 which, although similar to that of the 924 Turbo, employed lightweight cast alloy lower A-arms at the front, and stronger aluminium alloy semi-trailing arms at

The 924S as it appeared when introduced at the 1985 Frankfurt Show.

the rear. Oddly, despite the increased performance, only a 20mm front anti-roll bar was specified as standard, the thinner rear one having quietly found its way back onto the 924 options list about four years earlier in the UK. A slightly thicker front anti-roll bar was available, along with a 14mm diameter item for the back end and uprated shock absorbers.

The braking system was also inherited from the 944, so included ventilated discs with floating calipers on all four wheels; the discs themselves were 283mm diameter at the front, 289mm at the rear. Steering was via rack-and-pinion, with just 3.2 turns lock-to-lock, with or without power-assistance, while the handbrake was still sited between the driver's seat and the sill.

The body structure was basically the same as the old 924 (the only noteable change was the '924S' decal on the tail and the lack of rain gutters), but it now carried a ten-year anti-perferation warranty. However, new wheels and tyres distinguished the latest model from its predecessors. The attractive cast alloys had 6J rims (the 944 items looked similar but were, in fact, seven inches wide), and came mounted with 195/65 VR15 rubber.

The dashboard and interior was also largely carried over to keep down production costs, so what with the 944 being updated recently, there was quite a difference between the two. The familiar 380mm, three-spoke steering wheel came as standard, with the slightly smaller four-spoke item listed as an option. Overall weight was quoted as being 2578lbs (1172kg), with distribution being 51% front, 49% rear.

The 924S in Europe

In September, 924S prices started at £14,985 (the contemporary 944 was £18,234). There was no Lux variant this time, but the optional automatic transmission added a massive £1055. Add options such as leather seats, bigger 928S-style 16-inch wheels and tyres, power steering, a rear anti-roll bar, central locking, a sunroof, passenger door mirror, a stereo system, matching door panels, and so on, and it became a very expensive motor car.

Timing could have been better as, in mid-1985, Volkswagen had launched the 16v version of the Scirocco GTi. With 139bhp on tap in a lighter body, performance was easily on a par with that of the Porsche newcomer but, on the UK market, it cost a substantial 35% less than the basic 924S.

The only saving grace, as far as performance car makers were concerned, was that oil prices plummeted in 1986. Cheaper oil equals cheaper petrol, which tends to boost sales of larger-engined machines. However, Germany's latest emissions regulations came into force in January 1986, stipulating a requirement that all new vehicles use three-way catalytic converters to avoid a hefty pollution tax. It was an interesting development, but the lack of unleaded fuel in other parts of Europe made rather a mockery of it, and it was no coincidence that the basic price of a 944 in Germany, after it was equipped with a 'cat', rose by 7%.

So, what did the press think? Most loved the engine. The *Autocar* said that "the Porsche unit is one of the best four-cylinders in the world. It's magic, so silky smooth that drivers think it's a 'six'. It's marvellous, producing superb low-speed torque, great for poodling around town with virtually no revs in top, yet ultra-flexible, pulling from low-speed all the way up to the 6400rpm red-line with nary a falter."

Over at *Motor*, it was pretty much the same story. The headline ran: "A Porsche designed engine gives the Stuttgart baby the power it always wanted."

166

A UK specification 924S.

Below: Another view of the British model, complete with highly-desirable 'private' number plate. In fact, the registration dates back to 1977, but UK law stipulates that an earlier, age-related number is permissible; a later registration number on an older car is not.

The *Motor* test confirmed that, as usual, Porsche's figures were on the conservative side; testers clocked a 135mph top speed, 0-60 in just 7.8 seconds, and a 16.1 standing-quarter. Equally impressive was the 22.8mpg fuel consumption, an average borne out in several other road tests of the time.

But it wasn't all good news. A number of testers complained about backache, and the rather austere cabin, given the car's purchase price. The *Autocar* also noted: "Chassis aspects of the 924S disappoint ... there is too much rubberiness in the steering, attended by a lack of castor and consequent self-centring and, worse and most surprisingly from this manufacturer, a clearly detectable amount of bump steer."

In all fairness, the testers at *Motor* were happy and disappointed in equal measure, praising the steering, handling and balance of the machine. Interestingly, it stated: "Low speed ride is lively but no worse than you would expect from a sports car," although poor bump-thump and road noise suppression was still a point of issue, and the low-set steering wheel continued to be a major gripe.

Comparing the 924S with the turbocharged Mitsubishi Starion,

Standard coachwork colours (1986 MY)
Black, Pastel Beige, Guards Red, Copenhagen Blue, Alpine White.

Special coachwork colours
Graphite Metallic, Garnet Red Metallic, Kalahari Metallic, Stone Grey Metallic, Crystal Green Metallic, Sapphire Metallic, Mahogany Metallic, Zermatt Silver Metallic.

Trim materials
Black, Brown or Light Grey leatherette with matching inlays. Alternatively, inlays could be in Pinstripe velour (Black with White, Brown with Beige or Light Grey with White); seat facings could also be supplied in Pinstripe flannel cloth (in the same shades as the velour inlays), Black, Brown or Light Grey 'Porsche' cloth or leather as an option. Carpets came in Black, Brown, Burgundy or Light Grey.

A series of factory publicity shots showing the new car.

What Car? declared the Stuttgart car the winner in four of the six test categories, concluding that "the 924S has that welcome feel of solidity about it, coupled with a genuine air of quality. The Starion has a lot going for it but in the end the Porsche ranks as the more satisfying long-term prospect, both dynamically and financially."

Motor Sport summed up the new model thus: "Previously unexciting coupé has been brought alive by its refined new engine. Enjoyable handling and performance combined with a practical layout make for desirability. Expensive option list too easily levels cost up with more powerful stablemate."

The 924 returns to the US

In the November 1985 issue of *Road & Track*, John Dinkel wrote: "I've heard the same story so many different times recently I have to believe it's more than a rumour. Porsche is about to reintroduce the 924. That's right, the 924.

"Let me begin at the beginning. Start with the 928S. It recently received a four-valve version of its 4.7 litre V8. If you remember that the 944 engine is basically half that V8, then it doesn't take a genius to figure out that a 944S has got to be right around the corner. The four-valve 944S will put out about 180bhp compared with 143 for the current normally-aspirated 944. Naturally, the 944 Turbo will get the four-valve head, again with a commensurate increase in performance from its current 220bhp up to what I'd estimate would be 250-260.

"But now it all gets very interesting. Porsche resurrects the 924 body, stuffs in the two-valve 944 engine and, presto, an affordable Porsche. One that I'm told will sell for around $16,000. And won't that cause some alarm in the Mazda RX-7 ranks?

"Don't look for this revamped 924 – frankly, I think the 924 name is a mistake and Porsche should come up with something else – before the 944S is introduced. Reason? The 924 body is slippier than the 944's, and with equal engines the 924 would be faster, which would be bad for Porsche's image. When will all this happen? Not much before late 1986 is my best guess."

The 924S was duly introduced to the American market in June 1986 as an early 1987 model, priced at $19,900, and including air conditioning, electric windows and power mirrors as standard. Interestingly, in order to cut production costs, the aluminium alloy suspension pieces were left off 924Ss destined for the USA.

Enlarged bumpers and side markers were again necessary to comply with Federal regulations, and there was a high-level auxiliary brake light in the back window, so it was easy to tell a US specification car from a left-hand drive European one.

In US trim, with a 9.7:1 compression ratio, the 924S engine developed 147bhp at 5800rpm and 140lbft of torque at 3000rpm – the same figures as those for the 944. In addition, the gear ratios and final-drive were now exactly the same as European 924S models (US cars had a 016K gearbox), so, with the increase in power and not a great deal of additional weight to carry, the 924S could now eclipse the normally-aspirated RX-7 with ease in the performance stakes – a sub-16 second standing-quarter time was very impressive in the States.

Steering was geared to give 3.6 turns lock-to-lock, with power-assistance as standard. The wheels and tyres were the same as those found on European cars, so cornering power was fairly prodigious, two separate magazines recording 0.80g on the skidpan. But a 0-60 time of 7.8 seconds and a 134mph top speed (*Car & Driver* actually managed 7.5 and 136mph) soon put the increased performance into perspective. In America, the 924S was a fraction faster than a 944!

Road & Track listed the "much better 944 engine, good acceleration, [and] excellent handling feel" as its plus points, with the "old 924 dash looks cheap, steering wheel position too low, [and] unsupportive seats" being the main criticisms.

Writing for *Car & Driver*, Csaba Csere summed up the 924S as follows: "Some of the faithful may hesitate at

British advertising from 1987 showing (clockwise from top left): the 924S, the 16v 944S, the 944 Turbo, and the standard 944.

first, concerned that the S is a dead ringer for one of the pretenders of the past. But the true believers, who cherish performance above all else, will conclude that its superb balance, beautiful driving qualities, and high-speed capabilities make the new 924S worthy of wearing the Porsche crest."

By the end of the year, no less than 3096 had been sold there, a figure which represented 10% of Porsche sales in the US for '86. As a matter of interest, Porsche Cars North America Inc. announced it was hoping to sell around 5000 units a year in the future.

The 1987 model year proper

For 1986, 944s bound for the States got an increase in compression ratio (from 9.5 to 9.7:1), thus boosting power by 4bhp to 147 at a slightly higher engine speed (5800rpm), while torque went up from 137 to 140lbft, again at a useful 3000rpm. For 1987, a new timing belt pre-tensioner was fitted to reduce maintenance.

In the UK, things continued pretty much unchanged. Cars were still fitted with a front anti-roll bar only, but came with driving lights, tinted glass, a rear wiper, headlight washers, electric mirrors, and a leather-covered steering wheel as standard. Power steering was still an option on manual models, but standard on those with automatic transmission.

For the 1987 model year, the five-speed 924S was a whopping £18,464. By comparison, the basic 944 wasn't so different at £22,864, but the 944 Turbo was far from cheap at £34,168. Porsche prices in general now ranged up to £90,000 – the price of a decent house!

Boardroom drama

In America, sales of all German cars

A German-registered 924S for the 1987 model year.

Below left: A 924S fitted with the optional – and very expensive – 928S-style forged alloy wheels. These came with 205/55 VR16 tyres.

Another view of the 924S running on 16-inch alloys.

173

suffered in 1987. Although figures for the 924S were off by only 3% compared with 1986, this was actually a disaster, as the model was only sold for half of that year. The main reason for this poor showing was the strong deutschmark, the value of which had increased by 23% against the dollar in just 12 months.

At the end of 1987, in the wake of dwindling profits, a press release stated: "The Supervisory Board of Dr Ing. h.c. F. Porsche AG has announced that Mr Peter W. Schutz and Porsche AG have mutually agreed that Mr Schutz will resign from his position as Chairman of the Executive Board effective 31 December 1987.

"Mr Heinz Branitzki, Deputy Chairman of the Executive Board since 1976, was elected by the Supervisory Board yesterday [16 December] to be the new Chairman of the Executive Board as of 1 January 1988."

Schutz was determined to save the 911, which he did very successfully, but he also allowed the company to become almost reliant on the American market. Although the US market had always been immensely important, Ferry Porsche had quite deliberately kept its share of production under 50%, as he didn't want to rely too heavily on sales in one country. Over 60% of production was destined for America by the end of Schutz's tenure, and, with an unfavourable exchange rate, this was a disastrous situation which happened to coincide with the stock market crash, an additional problem

for the luxury car maker.

As for world economy, no-one could blame Schutz for that – it's worth noting that the events of October 1987, at least in percentage terms, were twice as bad as those of the Wall Street Crash of the late-1920s. And we all know what that led to. The future looked grim, but Ferry Porsche was positive that there was still a market for the Stuttgart thoroughbreds.

Interestingly, rumours of Schutz's departure had been circulating around the industry for some time, and in some quarters Ferdinand Piech was being put forward as his possible replacement. Ironically, despite his close links with Porsche through previous experience and family bloodlines, Piech was officially made Chairman of Audi on the same day as Branitzki took up his new position.

The 1988 model year
For the 1988 model year, the price of all Porsche's four-cylinder models shot up in Germany, with the 924S going from DM45,955 to DM49,265 in the space of four months. Naturally, this had a calamitous effect on sales, at home and in export markets in particular.

Power-assisted steering was now standard on all cars, as was a Spacesaver spare (which made one wonder what all the fuss was about before in the UK); due to the reduced effort necessary to steer, the smaller, four-spoke wheel was now standard equipment.

The 1972 shake-up of Porsche management resulted in this man, Heinz Branitzki, being put in charge of the company's business and finance administration. In 1988, following Schutz's departure, he was appointed Chairman.

With a 944-type exhaust system, new pistons and a higher 10.2:1 compression ratio (bringing with it a requirement for 95 octane fuel), the engine now produced a healthy 160bhp at 5900rpm (at the same time, by standardizing pistons, the basic 944 had its power reduced to 160bhp), but in an era when people were becoming used to Japanese machinery offering

174

Standard coachwork colours (1988 MY)
Black, Guards Red, Azure Blue, Alpine White.

Special coachwork colours
Nougat Brown Metallic, Maraschino Red Metallic, Almond Metallic, Satin Black Metallic, Nile Green Metallic, Ocean Blue Metallic, Stone Grey Metallic, Zermatt Silver Metallic.

Trim materials
Black, Burgundy or Light Grey leatherette with matching inlays. Alternatively, inlays could be in Pinstripe velour (Black with White, Burgundy with White or Light Grey with White); seat facings could also be supplied in Pinstripe flannel cloth (in the same shades as the velour inlays), Black, Burgundy or Light Grey 'Porsche' cloth or leather as an option. Carpets came in Black, Brown, Burgundy or Light Grey.

more and more for less and less, many journalists questioned whether the 10bhp increase was worth the difference in price. Add the cost of options such as air conditioning (£1515), the Sport suspension pack (£735), Sport shock absorbers (£260 if bought separately), a limited-slip differential (£725), 16-inch forged alloys with 205/55 tyres (£2022), a sunroof (£1008), cloth seat inlays and door trim (£142), a tinted windscreen (£46) and metallic paint (£602), not to mention a decent stereo, and suddenly it becomes expensive.

In America, the engine gained 11bhp, the catalogues now quoting 158bhp at 5900rpm and 155lbft of torque at 3000rpm. These figures represented a significant improvement, but, in Europe, peak torque was now very much higher up the rev-range, so the character of the car was quite different. It now had to be driven quite enthusiastically to get the best out of it – no problem with a manual gearbox, but far from ideal if automatic transmission was specified. Indeed, the official 0-60 time was put at a rather pedestrian 9.5 seconds!

However, there was a much greater problem. The price increase in Germany now put the basic 924S at $24,935 – after a few options had been added, this made it about the same price as a hard-charging Maserati Biturbo. The competition from Japan was very strong: the Nissan 300ZX Turbo, Mitsubishi Starion Turbo, Mazda RX-7 (either in Turbo or leather-trimmed convertible guise) and Toyota's Supra Turbo were all significantly cheaper, but offering reliable high-performance and a well-equipped cockpit.

In the UK, *Autocar* found the 1988 model year 924S could sprint from 0-60 in eight seconds dead, and go on to a top speed of 134mph. It could – fortunately – stop just as well, but with the increased performance (and weight – the 924S now weighed in at 2629lbs, or 1195kg) made the Porsche thirstier for fuel. Compared with the 1986 equivalent, the 22.6mpg average was 10% higher.

Car magazine had the following to say about the new car: "This year, as last, changes are few. Chief among them are to make power steering a standard fitment, and to boost the engine's power output by 10bhp by raising its compression ratio. That brings the total to 160bhp, the same as for the 944, whose output actually drops slightly from last year's 163bhp. The 924's torque is also up, from 140lbft to 155 at 4500rpm. The aim is to standardize engines and outputs.

"The power boost is claimed to raise the top speed by 3mph to 137mph and shave 0.3 seconds from the 0-62mph time, reducing it to 8.2 seconds, which isn't bad for a 2.5 litre coupé, but not so good for one costing £21,031.

"Those who step straight from the old 150bhp 924 probably won't have much trouble detecting this year's extra strength, even if it isn't apparent to someone who hasn't steered a 924 for a while. Either way, the 924 has the legs to mount a very brisk and satisfying advance across the countryside, but you won't be able to charge with quite the venom of the rider who saddles up in a Sierra Cosworth. The 924 simply isn't that fast – it is outpaced by machinery costing thousands less, even those shopping trolleys on steroids such as the Renault 5 GT Turbo. The 924 delivers poor performance per pound.

"You don't get many gizmos for 21-grand either. True, there are electric windows and door mirrors, but central locking is an extra, and, most incredible, so are cloth door inlays. Then you'll have to pay over £1000 for a hole in the roof. Still, this year's buyers will be able to console themselves with the discovery that they gain a headlamp levelling device and a cassette box incorporating a coin holder, both of which last year's 924 buyers had to manage without. And there's the chance to order a compact disc player, yours for £395."

In its summary of the 924S, *Motor* praised the "excellent performance and economy, smooth and flexible engine, good gearchange, well balanced chassis with exceptional traction, powerful brakes, [and] fine build and finish." However, it couldn't forgive the "high price, meagre standard equipment, dated fascia and instruments, awkward driving position, [and] mediocre ride."

Some were predicting that the 924/944 series could continue for another six or seven years, but with reviews like this and a flood of fresh

During the final few months of production polyurethane trim was fitted to the front spoiler area. It certainly tidied up the air intake area a little but, from a styling point of view, did tend to look rather heavy.

competition, combined with the news that production was being dramatically cut back (although rumours regarding Porsche abandoning the Neckarsulm works were fervently denied), it became increasingly obvious that, at the very least, the days of the 924S were numbered. There were still several developments outlined for the 944, but it was disturbingly quiet on the 924 front.

The limited edition 'Le Mans' model was announced following Porsche's 12th victory at the famous Sarthe circuit. With unique badging, a lowered suspension and 7J wheels at the back

(the standard 6J width was retained up front), only 980 were produced. A total of 500 black versions went to America, with the balance being finished in either black or white. In all, just 74 made it to Britain, 37 of each colour. From January 1988, the 924S was priced at £21,493, with the 'Le Mans' special being listed at £23,649 – just £1120 less than the 944, all of which were sold in Lux form in the UK, incidentally.

End of the line – part II
After a close shave in 1985, the 924 series was finally discontinued in July 1988. By early September 1988, the

924S was no longer listed in the UK, its final price being £21,923 for the five-speed manual version, or £22,903 for the automatic (by this time, the range had broken the magic £100,000 barrier).

For many, the 924S disappeared all too soon. True, production levels were low, but they were certainly much better than those of the 924 Turbo of earlier vintage. As one magazine said a little while later: "Gone, but not forgotten."

Just over 9000 of the 924S models were sold in America – more than half of the production run, whilst 1660

PORSCHE 924

924Ss were sold in the UK, taking British sales of the 924 series to a total of 11,270 units by the time production came to an end.

As a matter of interest, at the same time, the Volkswagen Scirocco fell by the wayside to make way for the new Corrado model. The 1.8 litre 16v model offered 131mph performance (0-60 came up in just 8.7 seconds), a 30mpg average and fine handling for just £16,700.

A *Motor* road test on the Porsche seemed to say it all – overall rating: eight out of ten, value rating: five out

of ten. In retrospect, with a new breed of cheaper competition coming onto the market, especially from Japan, perhaps it was just as well that the 924S retired gracefully when it did.

Was another 'cheap' model the way forward? A Porsche official noted: "It's a vicious circle. We want to build an affordable sports car. That means big volume and lots of proprietary parts. But as soon as you do that, the quality and prestige of the products suffers. We learned our lesson with the old Volks-Porsche 914, and with the original 924. Today, the management won't accept

any car unless it's 100% Porsche."

Although prototypes were built, ultimately, the amount of investment needed to get such a project off the ground – not just in terms of R&D, but a new factory to handle the level of production necessary to make it viable – simply didn't make commercial sense. A deciding factor was the strong deutschmark; having been around 3.5 DM to $1 at the start of 1985, three years later it stood at less than 1.7DM. In this price-sensitive end of the market, too many compromises would have to be made to keep costs down.

To match the front spoiler trim, the rear valance was given this undertray. It may be okay on the muscle-bound 944 Turbo, but looks somewhat out of place on the lithe 924 body. Production of the 924S ended in July 1988, thus bringing the 924 series to a premature end. However, more than 150,000 had been built during its 13-year run.

As the deutschmark continued to strengthen, Porsche decided to adopt a policy of becoming even more upmarket. Unfortunately, in order to see any kind of profit on cheaper models, prices in export markets had risen to such an extent that the cars were rendered uncompetitive. Although, for the vast majority, this took away the chance to realize a dream of Porsche ownership, in reality, it was the only logical answer.

8

BUYING & RESTORATION

In its day, the 924 suffered at the hands of the same unfounded snobbery as the 914 had before it, largely perpetuated by those who'd never even owned an example of the marque. Don't get me wrong, I think the 911 is a wonderful piece of machinery (my Uncle owns an ex-works RSR and a Kremer outlet – believe me, I know all about the mystique of the breed), but if one is to be brutally frank, the 911 was originally no more than a logical development of the 356, which, in turn, was a sporting development of the VW Beetle, another Porsche design.

Volkswagen has always been a part of Porsche heritage, so why try and hide it – the company itself was very open about the entire project. There was no disgrace in using proprietary engines and components, and Porsche was by no means the first of the top marques to do so. The big US and European conglomerates had been raiding the corporate parts bin for years in the interests of economies of scale, and development of the modular system further helped trim production costs.

Thankfully, the 914 has been universally accepted into the Porsche fold, and it looks at last as if the 924 is gaining recognition. *Popular Classics* stated: "The carved-from-solid feel common to all Porsches is there, only more so. The 924's amazing build quality is at its most impressive not so much when leaving the showroom, as some years, several owners and a considerable mileage later."

Power output from the normally-aspirated, two-litre engine was a long way from amazing, but it was adequate. However, brute force was never really part of the concept. If one was to cite a modern-day equivalent, it would have to be the Mazda MX-5 – a lightweight sports car that relies on a beautifully balanced chassis to provide enjoyment for the driver.

As Martin Buckley wrote for *Classic & Sportscar*: "Fifty-fifty weight distribution gives the 924 good, well-balanced handling that allows you to hold deliciously long drifts beyond the limit, though the normal attitude is neutrality with precise, informative and light steering – not unlike that of a 911 – allied to slight roll angles. For the money, it's really a lot of fun."

Following are a few brief pointers on what to look for when buying one.

Body

From the word go, the 924 came with an extensive six-year bodywork warranty, extended to seven years after 1980. Whilst many others struggled with the dreaded tin worm, Porsche could afford to do this because it had invested a vast amount of time, energy and money dealing with it before launching the car rather than trying to rectify a problem after the event.

Although some cars have suffered from rust, most well looked after examples should still be pristine. (Even after 20 years, my car had only one tiny rust spot on the top edge of the windscreen, and an owner's survey carried out in 1982 suggested a 92% success rate in beating corrosion.) The main reason for this is that Porsche applied a zinc coat at 500 degrees C

to galvanise the body, at first to just the lower sections but later the entire shell, inside and out.

Naturally, look for crash damage (the engine and transmission mounts can give a good indication of whether a car has been involved in an accident) and repairs, but on early models, check the door bottoms, the sills, around the door hinges, front wings and the airdam for signs of rust. In any case, if panels have been replaced, are they the proper galvanised items or cheaper substitutes?

The sunroof has been known to leak, so look for water marks and blockages in the drainage holes, and the fuel tank should be pressurised.

Exterior trim

What little there is generally of a very high quality, but expensive to replace if missing. Front bumper mountings on European specification cars are not particularly strong, so don't attempt touch parking with them.

Lots of parts came from the VW parts bin, but light lenses can be costly. For instance, because so many 924s have survived, second-hand driving light covers are apparently like gold dust. These are very susceptible to stone damage, and cost a fortune to buy through official channels.

The headlight motor is reliable, but the lights can be handwound into place if it fails. However, the 1982 survey suggested electrical faults (mainly the headlight switches and electric windows) were the 924's biggest problems, with almost half of the owners questioned reporting at least

one incident in two years. Compared to British and Italian cars from this period, that's hardly a significant figure, but it is worth remembering.

Remember to use two hands when closing the glass hatch, as abuse will lead to wear of the locating pins, which subsequently stops the panel seating properly. Water (and noise) can then enter the passenger compartment.

Engine

Original service schedules called for an oil and filter change every 6000 miles, with a full service every 12,000. As long as these have been adhered to, the 924 power unit should give years of faithful service. My car had covered 150,000 miles, started every time, never used any oil, was extremely economical and still had its factory oil pressure! Look after the engine, treating it with a dash of mechanical sympathy if it has a high mileage, and it will look after you.

If you think I'm being too kind, *Motor* was given a rare opportunity to test a 924 with over 100,000 miles on the clock. Compared with performance figures taken in 1979, the new times were almost identical, some actually a fraction in favour of the older car.

"100,000 miles and many millions of piston strokes have not blunted the pull of the 924's engine," *Motor* said. "Time and distance have done no harm to the engine at all, save a more frequent need to top up the oil sump. Surprised? So were we. Impressed? Ditto."

Obviously, carry out all the normal checks one would with a second-hand car, i.e. look for a smoky exhaust, signs

of a head gasket failure, check the compression, oil pressure, ask when the cam-belt was last changed, and so on. For those mechanically-challenged people looking to buy a car, the best advice is to consult an independent specialist or a local Porsche Club representative.

This goes double for the 924 Turbo, which can be very expensive to maintain. A blown turbocharger could cost as much as £1500 to replace by the time it has been fitted, so the faint-hearted should avoid this model at all costs. With the Turbo, a service record is an absolute must, and care should be taken not to push the engine when cold and to let it idle for a while before shutting it down.

The 924S is also going to be in a different league as regards maintenance. Again, demand to see the car's service history and get a specialist to inspect it. A little expense up front will potentially save a fortune a couple of years down the road. Just because the 924 is a sensible enthusiast's car, sadly, it doesn't follow that its previous owners were sensible enthusiasts ...

According to a buyer's guide from the *Autocar* in 1981, exhaust systems were not expected to last much beyond two years, particularly the back boxes. To replace a complete 924 system is cheap enough in the UK, but some exhaust components, particularly those relating to emissions equipment, can be fiercely expensive in the States. If one intends to keep the car for any length of time, it is probably worth investing in a stainless steel exhaust with a lifetime guarantee.

Transmission

Gearboxes are fairly robust, but older units will doubtless suffer a whine brought about by a tired pinion bearing; whining can also be induced by seizing clutch spigot bearings. A badly worn synchromesh is not going to be cheap to repair, so make sure the gearchange quality is good. Vibration in the propshaft can lead to a very expensive repair, and though a clutch is quite cheap to buy, the time needed to fit it can result in a nasty bill. Naturally, there should be no leaks from the transaxle unit.

Suspension, steering & braking system

The front brake discs have a reputation for wearing, and pad life is relatively short. Rear wheel bearings and brake adjusters are another weak spot, as is the top universal-joint on the steering column. None of these are particularly expensive to rectify, however. It may also be worth checking the rubbers on the rear suspension, as wear has a dramatic affect on handling.

Incidentally, rear hub nuts are outrageously tight – I had to go to a local truck dealer to get mine undone in order to replace the rear shoes! Bear this in mind when jacking up the vehicle: in other words, use axle stands – the leverage you need for this job could easily topple a car off a standard jack, which – after all, said and done – is only meant to be used for changing a wheel.

For those trying to run the car on a budget, many parts for the standard 924 can be sourced from cheaper outlets, as they originally came from the VW-Audi parts bin. However, components under this heading have a distinct bearing on safety, so avoid anything a mechanic wouldn't put on his own vehicle. Naturally, if it comes from a Porsche dealer, it's guaranteed to do the job properly, but will be much more expensive. Exercise a little common sense and caution – there is rarely such a thing as a true bargain!

Most of the tyres employed by the 924 range are freely available, and can be bought quite cheaply. Wheels are another matter, of course, but there's no shortage of people dealing in second-hand Porsche spares if money is tight.

Interior

Seats wear exceptionally well, but often split at the seams. This is fairly easy to remedy, and all the various trim materials are still available, albeit at a price. The seats have aluminium spacers underneath them, incidentally, and these can be taken out if you experience difficulty with the low steering wheel. Although only small, they do make a difference.

Dashboards often crack due to the sun drying out the plastic, and steering wheels have been known to do the same on occasion. Replacement is the only obvious but expensive answer, although in many cases, one may be able to source a good, second-hand one.

Fallen leaves tend to gather in the heater air plenum chamber in the scuttle area, which may block drainage vents if left unattended. Worse still, a blast from the heater's fan can leave the driver eating the leaves for breakfast!

Spares today

The German rule that requires spare parts to be manufactured for ten years after the end of a model's production run has ensured that most mechanical components are still available. Almost everything, except for the odd bits of trim, can be sourced at very reasonable cost. If one is willing to pay, it's fair to say that there isn't anything of note that cannot be bought at a Porsche dealership.

The best buy?

The standard 924 hasn't got an awful lot of power, but then it depends what you have been used to in the past, and the chassis is absolutely delightful. Most people seem to prefer the later five-speed gearbox, although the author rather liked the dog-leg first of the Getrag unit. One point of consensus; steer clear of the automatic unless your licence won't allow you to drive anything else.

The Turbo has great performance, but to go with its exotic turn of speed there are exotic maintenance bills. This model should not be regarded as a "poor man's Porsche" – make sure this is the car you want, as long-term running costs can be much the same as for a 911. If the combination of horsepower, a pretty shape and practicality are your reasons for ownership, go for it, but do so with your eyes open.

The 924S has a lot to offer, as I still prefer the 924 body to that of the 944, but also like the idea of more power without the frailty of the Turbo. But good examples hold their price, and many other vehicles can

Cutaway drawing of an early normally-aspirated 924 showing the positioning of all the major components. There were many changes over the years, including two completely different engines, but the basic concept remained the same throughout production.

look, but the standard 924 definitely offers the best overall value. The advice, as always, is buy the best example you can afford, as it will save money in the long run. Join a Porsche Club, and enlist its help to make sure the car is worth its asking price. Spending on club membership is an investment which will pay dividends in time – the chance to speak to fellow owners who've had similar problems, the route to cheaper spares, and a must nowadays for a lot of agreed value, classic car insurance policies.

I'll leave the final word to Paul Horrell of *Supercar Classics*: "People rule them out because the 944 has the better engine and a more brutal aspect. But a nice unblown 924 can be had for the price of a rock-bottom 944, and the 924 Turbo goes a lot harder than the 944 that supplanted it in Porsche's price lists. But to compare them with other Porsches is to miss the point. That they are Porsches at all is what matters – only by remembering that can you square their robustness with the amount of fun they deliver."

provide the same level of performance and handling much more cheaply. Of course, a Porsche is a Porsche, and for enthusiasts of the marque, nothing else can give that special feeling when you slip behind the wheel. But, again, with the expenditure needed to secure one, this is a car you have to really want and could only be justified if it was for everyday use.

As for prices, well, they seem to vary wildly depending on where you

PORSCHE 924

APPENDIX
PRODUCTION DETAILS

For production vehicles, the model years are used for dates, whereas competition models and specials are shown with calendar years. The chassis numbers shown are the first in each batch – apart from the competition models section (which include all the Carreras), they ran consecutively thereafter.

924

MY	Prod.	Notes	Chassis No.
1976	5145	Europe	9246100001
1977	25,656	Europe/RoW	9247100001
		US	9247200001
		US (1977.5 MY)	9247230001
		Japan	9247300001
		Japan (1977.5 MY)	9247330001
1978	21,562	Europe/RoW	9248100001
		US	9248200001
		Japan	9248330001
1979	20,619	Europe/RoW	9249100001
		US	9249200001
		Japan	9249330001
1980	12,794	Europe/RoW	92A0410001
		US	92A0430001
1981	11,824	Europe/RoW	ZZZ92ZBN400001
		US	AA092-BN450001
1982	10,091	Europe/RoW	ZZZ92ZCN400001
		US	AA092-CN450001
1983	5919	Europe	ZZZ92ZDN400001
1984	4659	Europe	ZZZ92ZEN400001
1985	3214	Europe	ZZZ92ZFN400001

924 Turbo

MY	Prod.	Notes	Chassis No.
1979	1932	Europe	9249400001
		US	9249500001
1980	5243	Europe/RoW	93A0140001
		US	93A0150001
1981	3312	Europe/RoW	ZZZ93ZBN100001
		US	AA093-BN150001
1982	1819	Europe/RoW	ZZZ93ZCN100001
		US	AA093-CN150001
1983	310	Italy	ZZZ93ZDN100001
1984	86	Italy	ZZZ93ZEN100001

924S

MY	Prod.	Notes	Chassis No.
1986	3536	Europe	ZZZ92ZGN400001
1987	8930	Europe/RoW	ZZZ92ZHN400001
		US	AA092-HN450001
1988	4193	Europe/RoW	ZZZ92ZJN400001
		US	AA092-JN450001

924 competition models

Year	Prod.	Type	Chassis No.
1979	16	SCCA Racer (NA)	92A0490001
1980	4	Le Mans Racer (T)	924001
1980	406	Carrera GT (T)	ZZZ93ZBN700001
1981	59	Carrera GTS (T)	ZZZ93ZBS710001
1981	17	Carrera GTR (T)	ZZZ93ZBS720001

Total 924 production **121,483**
Total 924 Turbo production **12,702**
Total 924S production **16,659**
Total competition model production **502**

Total series production **151,346**

Also from Veloce Publishing –

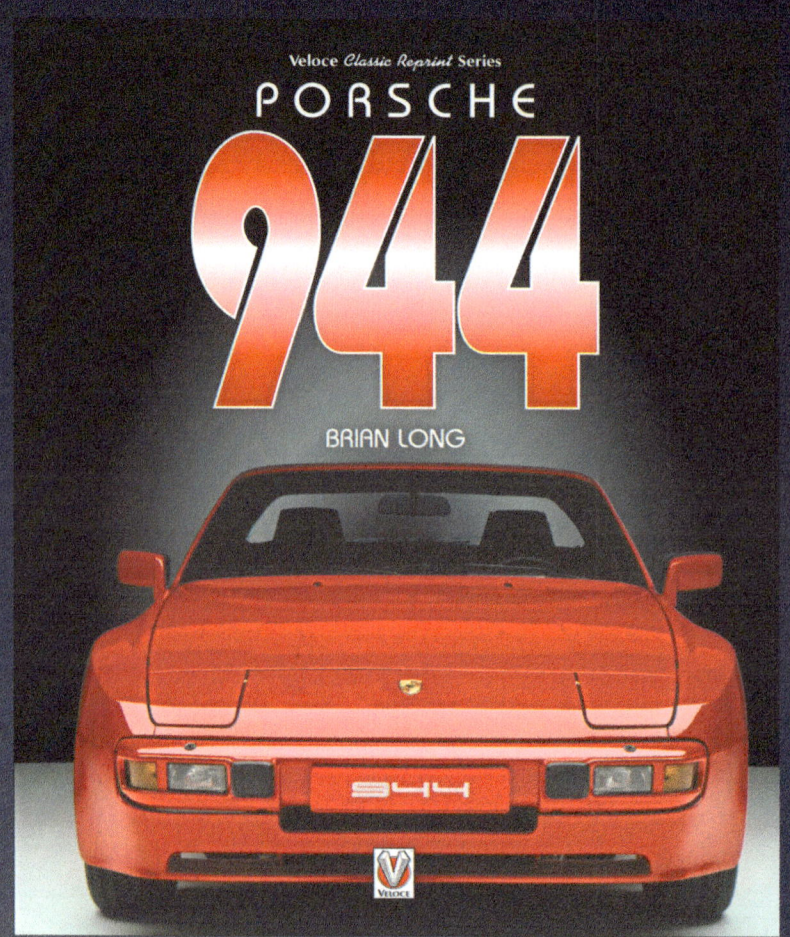

The definitive history of the 944 by an acknowledged expert. The 944 was introduced in time for the 1982 model year to fill the gap between the 924 and 928, and quickly became the fastest-selling Porsche of all time. Production of the 944 series ended in mid-1991, when the 968 took the model's place in the Porsche line-up.

ISBN: 978-1-845849-76-4
Paperback • 25x20.7cm • £35* UK/$60* USA • 192 pages

For more info on Veloce titles, visit our website at www.veloce.co.uk
email: info@veloce.co.uk • Tel: +44(0)1305 260068
* prices subject to change, p&p extra

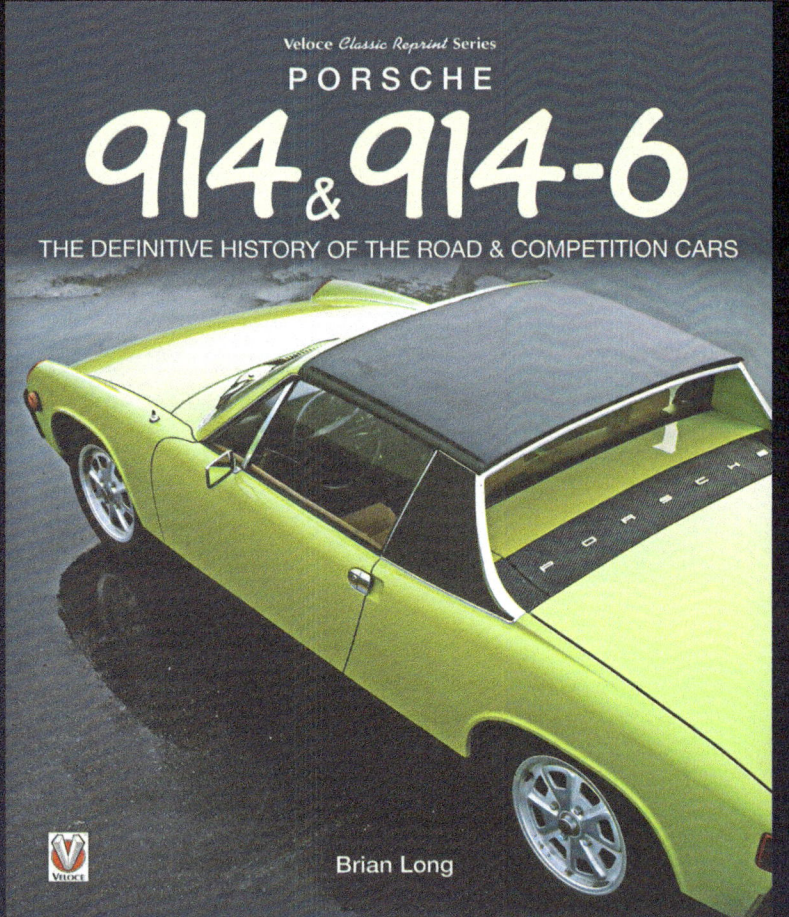

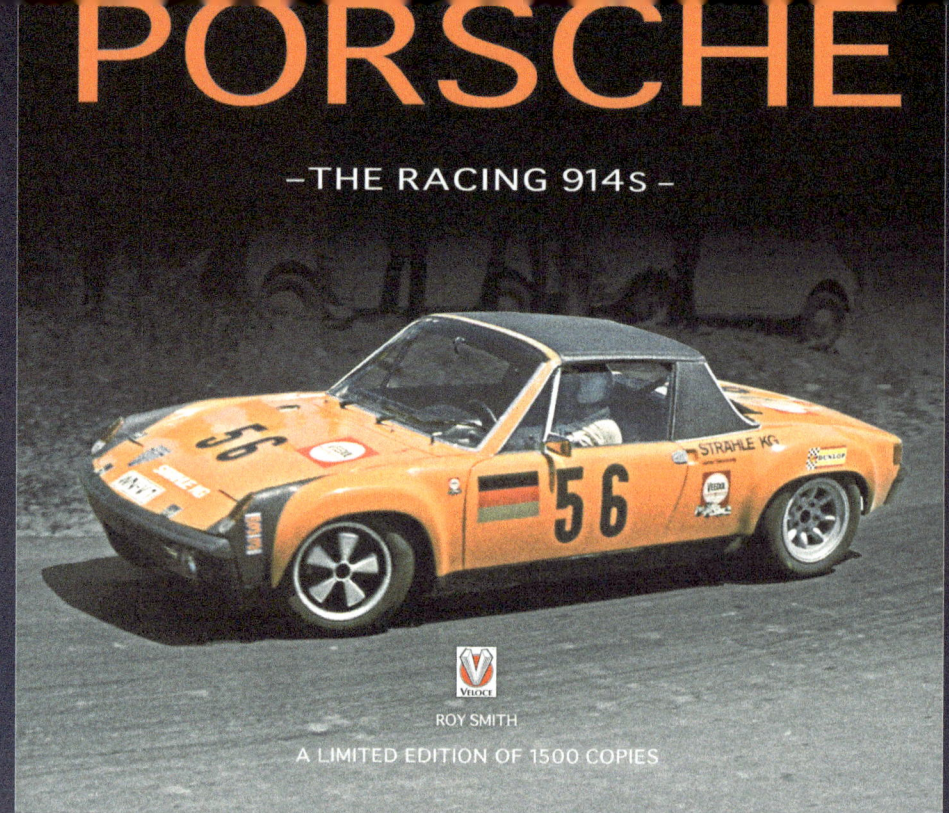

PORSCHE

– THE RACING 914s –

ROY SMITH

A LIMITED EDITION OF 1500 COPIES

Detailed study of a remarkable little car that, when it appeared in 1969, was considered a mish-mash of ideas, and not a 'proper' Porsche. It's also the story of the 'little' guys … the privateers and dealer teams who did most of the development that turned the 914 into great little racer.

ISBN: 978-1-845848-59-0
Hardback • 24.8x24.8cm • £65* UK/$120* USA • 320 pages • 452 colour and b&w pictures

For more info on Veloce titles, visit our website at www.veloce.co.uk
email: info@veloce.co.uk • Tel: +44(0)1305 260068
* prices subject to change, p&p extra

INDEX

*The Porsche company and its products
are mentioned throughout the book.*